Revitalize
Author: Chelli Guthrie
Editor: Erin McDonald
Graphic Designer: Elisa Elmshaeuser

Kaio Publications Copyright 2017

*To my parents for giving me close family ties
and a love of learning that I wanted my children to have.*

The Origin of It All

As of this writing, our family is beginning our eighth year of homeschooling. None of my children have ever attended public or private school despite my personal history as a teacher. I would love to say that I was convicted by my time in the classroom to homeschool, but I was not. I had the mindset of many educators and the general populace about homeschooling, that it was a choice certain to ruin your children and make them social outcasts. The idea of homeschooling my own children was laughable, but two events occurred to change everything.

First, I met and observed two families who broke all of the misconceptions I believed about homeschooling. Second, when I returned to the classroom briefly as a substitute teacher, things had changed in the public school system, and not for the better. I could no longer imagine placing my sweet three-year-old daughter into that environment in a couple of years. I came home that day and told my husband I wanted to try homeschooling. Thankfully, he had been enthusiastic about the idea for quite some time.

I jumped in eager and confident, but it didn't take too long for me to realize homeschooling was a much more complicated and stressful situation than I'd imagined and one for which my teaching degree had not prepared me. This book is rooted in my years of homeschooling and struggling to homeschool in a way that empowered my children and left me feeling satisfaction at the end of the day. Many times I was driven to the Bible because I didn't know what to do. Often I felt I was floundering and failing at this homeschool experiment, with only one shot to get it right.

On the following pages you will find a compilation of my own personal study that came out of those times of distress and the lessons I've learned and am still learning. I feel most inadequate to be regarded as an expert on this topic or having it all together. I still struggle with many of the challenges in this book, and at this point, I am certain I will never stop struggling. What has changed, though, is my mindset, and that is my desire for you as you read and work through these devotions. I'm not attempting to create the perfect homeschool in your home. Instead, I want to walk beside you and help you renew your mind and your confidence about homeschooling. We can be students together.

Dosing Instructions

This book is divided into two main sections: Weeks You are Homeschooling and Weeks You are Not Homeschooling. In the Weeks You are Homeschooling section, you will find thirty-six weeks of devotionals to correspond with the most common homeschool year breakdown. In the Weeks You are Not Homeschooling section, you will find an additional sixteen weeks of devotionals to round out the calendar year.

While you are free to use the book any way you wish, even reading straight through it, it is designed to be read over the course of the year. Every Sunday or Monday read the devotional, and answer the questions that follow. Over the course of the week, work on the Prescription, or challenge, issued at the end of each entry. Don't stress if you don't complete one, just keep going. The devotionals to be read during the weeks you are homeschooling will have challenges focused on your homeschool and/or your children. The devotionals during the weeks you aren't homeschooling will be focused on you and your mindset.

Remember, no one, including myself, does everything in this book well or successfully. However, God is on our side. He wants us to succeed in educating our children. I pray this book will be a tool to help you do exactly that. Have a great year!

Chelli

For the Weeks You Are Homeschooling

Week 1

For the one who doubts is like a wave of the sea that is driven and tossed by the wind. For that person must not suppose that he will receive anything from the Lord; he is a double-minded man, unstable in all his ways. —James 1:6b-8

A few years ago I had a panic attack about homeschooling. A storm of uncertainty and despair rained down on me. Doubts began to take over my thoughts. Fears began to paralyze me: "Will my children be prepared for college? What if they don't go to college, will they be prepared for that possibility? What if I forget to teach them something they needed to know and it ruins their life? What if we should be studying Chinese, like that other homeschool family? Should I add more subjects to our homeschool day? It seems like we do too little. Should I get rid of some subjects? Our day seems too long."

Doubts and fears about our choice to homeschool sent me down rabbit trails for the perfect curriculum to alleviate my misgivings. I looked to other homeschool families as my example of what to study with my own children and how to schedule our days. I questioned everything about our homeschool wondering if it was good enough. Finally I couldn't take it anymore; this line of thinking was driving me insane. Like a dog chasing its tail, I had no direction in our homeschool. I had no clear cut goals. I had nothing to direct our studies except external curriculum and comparisons to what others were doing. What was I supposed to do now?

I found my answer in the above verses one morning during my Bible study time. In front of me, in black and white, was exactly the problem with our homeschool. I had doubts about what I was doing and whether I was capable of doing it. I was being driven and tossed about by every new wind of homeschooling methodology or curriculum that came along. I was double-minded. I was unstable. And because of this, there was no way our homeschool would receive any blessing from the Lord. The Lord can't be glorified with wishy-washy. The Lord can't be honored with doubt.

The need to restore sanity and peace to my mind and our homeschool forced me to my knees in prayer and develop a vision statement for my children's education. Creating a vision statement has been the single, best thing I've ever done for our homeschool. No matter the path we take in our homeschool, I know the results I want to achieve at the end. Having a vision statement allows me to focus everything we do, to test and see if our routine, curriculum, and extracurricular activities each support and further the hopes we have for our children. God is glorified in God-honoring goals, and He is honored in a heavenly direction in our homeschools.

I spent time envisioning what my children would look like as adults embarking upon their own lives and journeys away from our home and protection; children who would make our time homeschooling a success. I wrote ideas down, I erased some, I crossed out others, I prayed, I talked with my husband, and finally I had our vision statement. Here is our "Big Three," as I like to call them, our homeschool mission statement:

Love God and Others

In all that I do, I consider how I can help my children love God and love other people more and more. Our world needs love, kindness, gentleness, and patience. I want my children to be the next generation to pass that on to others while growing in their own relationship with God. I want them to be exposed to and interact with as many races, religions, cultures, and ideologies as possible so they can understand and love their fellow man who are made in His image.

Know How to Learn

My fears and doubts that my children might not know something they need when they graduate high school is absolutely assured. They will encounter information they need to know, but do not. The key is to make sure they know how to learn, how to find information, how to understand that information, and how to assimilate that information to previous knowledge.

Be Effective Communicators

Whatever job or profession our children have, they will need to be able to communicate with someone about something. I want my children to be good, concise writers as well as someone who can speak to a group of people. I want them to be able to share their feelings and needs to friends and family seasoned with love and respect.

This vision statement drives all of my homeschool decisions and curriculum choices. If I feel a specific curriculum, approach, or activity will help my children achieve these three goals, I take a closer look. If the answer is no, I can walk away without anxiety or doubt. I don't feel out of control or stuck on a roller coaster of insanity anymore.

Diagnosis:
Have you ever had those questions of doubt and fear about being a successful homeschooler? What were they?

Why does having a vision statement help keep you free from anxiety and doubt about what you are achieving in your homeschool?

Prescription:
You know what this challenge will be! Spend some deep time in thought and prayer about what you hope for your children at the end of your homeschool journey. What will make you feel successful as a homeschool mom? What would make them successful homeschool graduates in your eyes? Obviously my homeschool's vision statement should and will be different from yours due to differences in family culture and family personalities.

One thing to note is that I didn't include mastery of subjects in our homeschool vision statement because I know that having my children achieve proficiency in math and reading is a given. Type or write your vision statement and place it in your personal files or a teacher binder. Refer to it often, maybe every week, to remind you that the end game is what is most important.

Week 2

And Jesus increased in wisdom and in stature and in favor with God and man.

—Luke 2:52

In recent years, I discovered the importance of setting goals to help keep me focused on what is important, especially in our homeschool. When so many new and shiny things come on the market, it's easy to be led astray from what is working in your homeschool. While it's important to set large, overarching principle goals, I also like to set specific, narrow goals every year for our homeschool and each child. I found this small verse referenced above about Jesus' childhood was the perfect template to make personal goals for my children each year because it really covers all areas of their lives.

Wisdom

This category refers to your academic goals for the year. It helps to be specific and have a plan to achieve them. For example, the wisdom goals for my children one year were as follows: my oldest child would learn her multiplication and division facts by playing a computer game five days a week for twenty minutes, my middle child would learn cursive by working through a cursive workbook and then writing all of her school assignments in cursive the rest of the year, my youngest child would learn his numbers 1-20 and his alphabet by working with me for fifteen minutes every day. When you set goals for school with measurable quantities like this, it's much easier to keep on track.

Stature

I write down physical and health goals for the year here. I usually create a family goal such as walk around the neighborhood at least four times a week and eat more fruit during the day. I also look at areas I feel the kids need to focus in each of their lives. It might be focusing on nutrition and what makes a healthy meal, or it could be needing to cross some physical education milestones off the list, like learning how to throw a ball correctly or running a mile.

Favor with God

These goals are your spiritual goals for the year. I do a pretty good job of teaching Bible knowledge to my children, but I realized about a year ago that I needed to focus on encouraging their personal relationship with God. I started focusing on teaching them how to study the Bible for themselves and slowly began encouraging them to do personal Bible study books on their own. Sometimes it's easy as a homeschooler to feel like your kids are getting lots of Biblical education because of how we can use curriculum that is religious based, but it's important to remember that they need goals focused on having one-on-one time with God as well.

Favor with Man
Probably known by its more common name of character training, this category's focus includes interpersonal relationship goals; or in other words, how to play nice with others. Generally these are the type of goals about being grateful, kind, respectful of property, obedient, and using uplifting speech, etc. I usually pick out one principle that I'd like each child to work on for the year. I have a one-on-one (no point in having siblings hear this!) chat with them to let them know specific behaviors that are encouraged and ones that are not. During the year, I try to really cheer them on when they demonstrate behaviors and attitudes that fit with what we talked about at the beginning of the year and if things seem to be falling apart for them in that area, we might need to have another one-on-one discussion with some consequences added for poor behavior.

As you can see, it really is the perfect verse to help focus on goals for your children (and for yourself!).

Prescription:
This week use Luke 2:52 as your guide to create yearly goals for your children in each of these four areas. Don't put too many goals under each category or you'll stress yourself out trying to achieve them all! I usually shoot for one or two in each category for each child. Put some time and thought into these. Be sure and keep your goals handy in your lesson planner or saved on your computer so you can refer back to them throughout the year. You'll be amazed how having a simple goal framework will keep you focused on what's important over the coming months.

Week 3

Do not be deceived: God is not mocked, for whatever one sows, that will he also reap. For the one who sows to his own flesh will from the flesh reap corruption, but the one who sows to the Spirit will from the Spirit reap eternal life. And let us not grow weary of doing good, for in due season we will reap, if we do not give up. —Galatians 6:7-9

What are you sowing in your homeschool? If you're not sure, then look at what is being reaped. For the past two lessons, we've discussed making an overall vision statement for your homeschool and personalized goals for each of your children. Now it's time to truly think about how to reap those goals. The verses above give us some direction in how to make it happen.

Prepare the Soil

If you've ever had a garden or flower bed, you know how important this step is. While you can go out and just throw some seed on the ground, the odds are not great that you will ever have anything grow, or if something does grow, it will be weak and unfruitful. The ground needs some assistance to be full of nutrients that help plants achieve their full potential, so many gardeners add fertilizer, compost, or manure to areas where they plan to plant. Likewise, our children need to be properly prepared before we ever begin to sow. Our children are not going to be receptive to our teaching or our goals for them if they are not prepared. We need children that listen to our instruction, respect us as parent and teacher, and with whom we have a loving relationship. If these three things are not present, then your soil is not ready, and you need to spend time preparing the soil before moving on to the next steps. (I'm going to only mention the conditions I believe need to be met to prepare the soil this week. There are other weeks in this book where these items are covered more in-depth.)

Be Intentional

Planting a garden or sowing seeds doesn't happen by accident. When I was growing up, my parents had a big garden every year. The garden didn't get planted on a whim. My mom first drew up a plan of what she wanted to plant in each location and how much of it she wanted to plant. Next, she gathered all the things she'd needs such as seeds, plants, tiller, hoe, etc. Finally, she informed all of us that the garden planning would take place on a specific day so that we would all be available to help.

Sowing seeds with your children to reap the goals you have created for them is exactly the same. I'll use the first part of my family vision statement I shared in Week One as an example. If my goal is to have children that love God and others, then I need to teach them how to handle conflict that could lessen or destroy that love, how to show love to God and others in an appropriate way, how to develop a relationship with God and others via time spent together and communication.

For each of these items, I would need to be intentional about how to teach each of these as well. How am I going to teach them how to handle conflict with parents, siblings, friends, etc.? Do I need some help in that area myself before I can teach my children? How are we supposed to show love to God? Are there passages in the Bible that tell us? How can I teach this to my children? How are we supposed to love others? What does loving someone look like? Do I love others the way I should, and do my children see that? Hopefully, you get the idea. This step in the process is the most time intensive, but necessary for successful reaping, because it gives you a plan.

Sow from the Spirit

As homeschool moms, sometimes it's easier for us to focus on the academic or intellectual benefits of the goals we have for our children more than the spiritual side. However, the verses above tell us that if we focus on the fleshly or worldly side of our goals, then corruption will be all that is reaped. The goals that we've made or the vision we've created will be corrupted into something not of God. When we are implementing experiences and ideas to help our children achieve their goals, it's so important to continuously point out how this will help them glorify God, help the church, and grow their faith. Don't emphasize the academic benefits or how it will look on their transcript or resume. The worldly benefits from achieving their goals will not even be an issue if they put God and His kingdom first (Matthew 6:33).

Persevere

In case you didn't know this already, you have to teach your children things more than once for them to truly learn. In fact, you may need to teach them the same lesson multiple times before they truly apply it and use it in their lives. Do not get discouraged when it seems your homeschool is not following the vision you have for it or when your child is not even close to achieving the goal you set for them this year. The devil wants you to get discouraged and give up so that those life-changing, God-honoring goals you have for your children will never be realized. After having three children, I've consistently struggled with my weight. I also am a perfectionist, so for a long time I didn't attempt to lose weight because I was afraid I couldn't lose all of it. My husband pointed out that even if I only lost half the amount I wanted to, it would still be a victory because at least I'd lost something. Goals and homeschool visions are the same. If you set the goal for your child to learn all of their addition facts through twenty this year, but it looks like they will only learn the ones through ten, then rejoice in that! They might not have reached the goal, but they've succeeded.

The amount of wonderful blessings that I want to reap in my homeschool and in each of my children's lives is incalculable, and I know you feel the same. Ultimately, though, it will not be by our efforts or our talents if even one of these goals comes to pass. We may sow, others may come along who help water (Bible class teachers, mentors, ministers, etc.), but ultimately God gives the increase (1 Corinthians 3:6).

Diagnosis:

If someone was spying on your family for one week, what seeds would they think you are sowing in your homeschool? Earthly seed (focused on earthly success) or spiritual seed (focused on Godly success)? Godly character or not sowing character at all?

Do you get discouraged when your children do not seem to be progressing as quickly as you would like at the goals you set for them? What do you think God might be trying to teach you in those situations?

Prescription:

This week, choose one of your items from your homeschool vision statement or one of your child's individual goals, and go through the planning steps of being intentional. Brainstorm a list of questions about that goal or vision and what needs to be taught to achieve it. Distill it down into a quantifiable, teachable goal or vision. Now find ways to implement it. When it comes to goals about character (such as my example above about love), usually it involves being aware and involved when the opposite happens in your family and intervening every time to help your children learn. When it comes to academic or physical goals, it is easier to quantify those and see improvement. Either way, keep on keeping on!

Week 4

For whatever was written in former days was written for our instruction that through endurance and through the encouragement of the Scriptures we might have hope.
—Romans 15:4

Have you ever wondered why God gave us the Bible? The verse above gives us two reasons: instruction and hope. Interestingly enough, I started a practice last year in our homeschool that proved to have the same effect. I began to journal about our homeschool day. Once or twice a week I would jot down a positive event or encouraging thought. Before I knew it, I had my own homeschool "Bible" of sorts to instruct and give me hope.

Instruction through Endurance

In case you didn't know this homeschool secret yet, I'm sharing it with you right now. You are going to encounter days, weeks, possibly even months where you are discouraged about homeschooling. All you can focus on is what is going wrong and how tired you feel when faced with the prospect of another day of homeschooling.

In situations like this, I've discovered my homeschool journal is the best medicine. I can pull it off the shelf, read some entries, and slowly feel a smile work its way across my face. It's a tangible reminder of endurance. Many of the weeks that I wrote an entry, I felt just as discouraged with homeschooling at that point, but I made wonderful memories and learned important lessons in spite of my feelings. My homeschool journal instructs me that I can endure discouragement and be successful.

Encouragement to Have Hope

Throughout my eight years of homeschooling, I have had moments where I was certain my children would never achieve some educational milestone. Basically I'd lost hope they would master fractions, learn to read, or even make it past the Middle Ages in history. Every day I could witness the ruination of any academic success; this only led me to anxiety and worry.

Capturing past academic achievements on paper in my journal encourages me to have hope. I find within its pages previous achievements that let me know my current struggles will not persist. All will be well if I remain patient and diligent, because I can read about our past successes and cling to the memories of my abilities as a teacher and the capabilities of my children.

Writing down my former days and having them at my perusal, has become such a special part of our homeschool that it is the one major regret I have. I wish I would have started from the beginning of our homeschool journey.

Diagnosis:
Why does it seem so easy to focus on the negative experiences in homeschooling and forget the positives?

In what ways could creating a record or journal of the happy and positive moments help you during the hard times?

Prescription:
Pick up a cheap journal or create a document on your computer and commit this homeschool year to writing an entry at least once a week of a memorable moment or an educational achievement you reached. Feel free to look back through this book as the year goes along for reminders of hope and endurance. My kids even like to flip through last year's book because it's a great encouragement to them as well.

Week 5

And he told them many things in parables, saying: "A sower went out to sow. And as he sowed, some seeds fell along the path, and the birds came and devoured them. Other seeds fell on rocky ground, where they did not have much soil, and immediately they sprang up since they had no depth of soil, but when the sun rose they were scorched. And since they had no root, they withered away. Other seeds fell among thorns, and the thorns grew up and choked them. Other seeds fell on good soil and produced grain, some a hundredfold, some sixty, some thirty." —Matthew 13:3-8

Teaching is a lot like sowing seeds; you throw out information and hope some of it takes root. The parable of the sower that Jesus tells is also a good reference on how to help our children truly learn.

The First Soil
Obviously we don't want this to be our children, but we must be careful. It's very easy to assume that kids are learning what we teach them, but children are very good at faking. Usually I see this happen in a homeschool setting when parents rely on computer-based learning for one or more subjects. Their child discovers how to cheat the system, and the parents are none the wiser until much later. I'm not criticizing learning via DVD, CD-ROM, or internet (I use some of these in our homeschool), but parents do need to be involved even when using a curriculum done solely by the student, or you may discover they haven't learned anything, and all that information has been devoured before it ever had a chance to be retained.

The Second Soil
I believe this soil is probably the vast majority of us who went to public or private school. It is the classic case of cramming definitions and information into our head the night before an exam, passing the test, and promptly forgetting almost everything. Ask us a week later for the parts of a plant cell and no one can remember despite earning a passing grade. This begs the question: did we really learn it? Does the grade we earned truly reflect our knowledge a week later? Hopefully we desire more from our homeschools than cramming facts into our children's head only for it to all be forgotten in a few days. In other words, there is no depth to this type of learning; it is shallow and easily withers away.

The Third Soil
In this case, you do learn something since it takes root, but you don't understand it, so it never is useful or fruitful in the student's life. Believe it or not, phonics was this subject for me. I taught myself to read when I was four and despite my first grade teacher's attempts, I never learned phonics because I didn't see the importance of what she was trying to teach me. Fast forward to when I began teaching my own children to read. I had no clue how phonics worked. I remember calling my mom

to double check what sound long "A" made! As I taught my own children, I discovered how interesting the English language really was, why certain letters and letter combinations made the sound they did in different words, different spelling rules, etc. I had the knowledge of what phonics was, how it worked, and even completed numerous worksheets about it, but I'd never used it. We definitely don't want our children to learn various subjects and then never be able to really use the information in different situations.

Diagnosis:
Have you had any experience with any of the three soils of learning above? Which ones?

What kind of learning would you like your children to have in your homeschool? Do you believe that is an attainable goal?

Prescription:
One of the best ways to see how well your child has learned something is to have them be the teacher. This week do a little bit of spot-checking to see how well your child is learning. Have each one teach something to you or to the family. You can choose the subject, but I suggest math or one of the language arts subjects. It will be pretty easy to tell how well they truly understand what they are doing. If they struggle to explain or get stuck while explaining, that's your clue that the learning in your home is failing in one of these three areas. Record below how each child does.

Week 6

Other seeds fell on good soil and produced grain, some a hundredfold, some sixty, some thirty. —Matthew 13:8

Last lesson I introduced the parable of the sower with a different viewpoint from the spiritual application Jesus gives: an academic application that has to do with learning. This week I want to zero in on the last type of soil and how we can take our children to a deep, working knowledge of what we teach that will produce fruit in their lives.

Distill it Down

One of the first things taught in my education classes in college was how to create a lesson plan. Before you ever begin working on activities or assignments, you determine what the objective or goal of the lesson should be. The same idea holds true for effective learning in our homeschools. When you begin a new subject or topic in your homeschool you need to decide what specifically you want your children to carry with them from the subject. For example, last year I did a very basic chemistry course with my kids. Before I ever started gathering resources, I decided that I wanted my children to learn the states of matter, that all things in the universe are made of atoms, the parts of an atom, how different elements interact and react with other elements, how compounds, mixtures, and solutions are formed, and the basic structure of the periodic table of elements. The beauty of having a focus like this before you begin your study is that it helps you review the information that you truly want your children to memorize. No one can remember everything, so choose a few facts that are most important and go over it throughout your school year.

Repetition is the Mother of Memory

No one likes to admit it, but the science backs it up; the more you repeat information, the more easily it is retained. There are many things we want our children to memorize for safety purposes (address, phone number), for academic purposes (math facts, grammar definitions, science facts), and for religious purposes (scripture, bible facts, tenets of our faith). I want my children to have a good general timeline of world history in their heads, so every year we read through a narrative book of world history, we keep a huge timeline on the wall in the hallway, sing a timeline song every morning, and one of our favorite games to play is called "Timeline," where you have to correctly put your timeline cards in order. What your family deems important enough to memorize is up to you, but one thing is certain, you will need to repeat, repeat, and repeat again that information to truly lock it in your child's long-term memory so it's available when needed. Of course memorization and repetition don't have to be boring. You can memorize loads of information through songs, chanting, playing games, acting, etc.

Get Out of Their Way

Even in states with strict homeschool laws, there is room for rabbit trails in your homeschool year. In fact, I would say that rabbit trails are necessary if you want to see the educational fruit mentioned in the above verse. Once you give your children the most important facts about what you are learning and once you've helped establish a pattern of memorizing information, then it will be time to get out of their way, because that is where the true growth in their education will begin. It's inevitable that something you are studying will trigger an interest in your child. For my oldest it's been mythology, for my middle child, it's been hieroglyphics, and for my youngest, it's all about nature and how the natural world works.

Too often as homeschool moms, I think we view these rabbit trails as deviating from our nicely laid plans or getting us off schedule, but the opposite is actually true. When your children find a passion or an interest for something, stop your regularly scheduled program and let them go. Why? Because this type of learning is exactly what we want to see in our children. It's what will produce the largest harvest in their lives. When children are naturally engaged in a subject, the importance and the memorization will happen on their own. Instead of pulling up those small plants of interest before they even have a chance to grow, sit back and watch the plentiful harvest.

Homeschooling our children is a sacrifice of time and money for most homeschool moms. It is not a very good return on this investment if our children remember very little of what we've invested all of our time and money into teaching them, or if the few times they did show an interest, we squelched it quickly.

Diagnosis:
Have you ever found yourself in a situation where you ask your children about a topic you've already covered in your homeschool and your child remembers nothing? How does that make you feel about the time and money you spent to teach that topic?

Do you teach information and move on, or do you come back periodically to review? Do you think reviewing would help your child to remember? Why?

Do you allow rabbit trails in your homeschool? Why or why not?

Prescription:
One of the best ways to see how well your child has learned something is to have them be the teacher. This week do a little bit of spot-checking to see how well your child is learning. Have each one teach something to you or to the family. You can choose the subject, but I suggest math or one of the language arts subjects. It will be pretty easy to tell how well they truly understand what they are doing. If they struggle to explain or get stuck while explaining, that's your clue that the learning in your home is failing in one of these three areas. Record how each child does.

Week 7

Rejoice always, pray without ceasing, give thanks in all circumstances; for this is the will of God in Christ Jesus for you. —1 Thessalonians 5:16-18

What does God want of you as a homeschool mom? What does He want of your children? It seems to be a tall order, but our homeschools should be characterized as joyful, prayerful, and thankful. We need to make it a point to practice these characteristics with our children daily.

Rejoice Always
It's easy to find yourself and your children falling into the rut of being Negative Nancys. The kids start responding that they hate certain subjects or that they are terrible at specific tasks. You begin to feel that the homeschool day is nothing but drudgery and count the seconds until it's over. Christians are not to be clouded constantly with an attitude of melancholy and negativity. We are commanded to rejoice!

Pray Without Ceasing
A homeschool full of prayer. It sounds wonderful and puzzling at the same time. Do you pray for your homeschool every day? Do your children pray about their school day as well? Praying without ceasing is not a time command, but a content command. If you are praying without ceasing, you are praying about everything; all of your actions, decisions, concerns, and people that you interact with during a day. Prayer is never removed from your homeschool, nor is it relegated to a specific prayer time during the day.

Give Thanks in All Circumstances
A Harvard Business Review article from 2013 looked at production output in the workplace and specifically what effect comments from superiors had on their employees. What they found was that the most productive teams had a ratio of positive to negative feedback of almost 6 to 1. In other words, it took about six positive comments to every one negative comment to keep the workplace running at its most effective. Many times, I believe thankfulness or gratitude is the same way. It is easy for us to fall into a habit of complaining and worrying, which can drag us down into the mire. It takes many more moments of thankfulness to pull us out again, which is probably why the Bible focuses so much on counting our blessings.

Joy, Prayer, and Thankfulness in Your Homeschool
Since we know that these are commands God expects of us as His children, we know the importance of modeling these traits in our homeschools and helping our children learn how to live them out. On the following page, let's take a quick look at each one on a practical level.

Joy: Instead of letting yourself or your children focus on the subjects or skills that cause frustration or dislike, put a positive, joyful spin on each interaction. When your child says, "I hate history," point out how much they've already learned about history or share an interesting fact from your history lesson that day. When it's time for math and you dread it as much as your child, take a joy break before beginning. Jump up, put on some fun music, and dance for five minutes before you start. Suddenly math is associated with a fun dance break instead of drudgery to finish. A simple shift in perspective does wonders for everyone.

Prayer: We always open and close our homeschool day with prayer, as probably many of you, but the concept of praying without ceasing was one I hadn't really implemented. It really stunned my oldest when she sat down for our math lesson one morning and I said, "Grace, we always struggle with doing math together. You become frustrated and I become frustrated that you are frustrated, which doesn't end well for either of us. Let's pray and ask God to help our attitudes and give us understanding before we begin today." Her eyes got wide in shock, but I went ahead and prayed for both of us. It wasn't a miraculous math lesson, but it was one where we stopped short of frustration and regained control, which almost never happens. I know it was because we'd prayed before beginning, and both of us had the Lord on our minds, and more awareness that He was there at the math lesson with us.

Thankfulness: After reading the book, *Raising Grateful Kids in an Entitled World*, this past summer, I instituted a new ritual to our homeschool day. As we close out, standing around the table, everyone has to share at least two things they are thankful for from that day. Initially, the children were very generic in their thanks. They were thankful for our family, Jesus, food, etc. I wanted them to go deeper than that, though, and really put some thought into their thanks to God. I began modeling being very specific with events that had occurred that day for which I was thankful, usually involving one of the children or my husband. I noticed that as I became more specifically thankful, so did the children. It is now one of their favorite parts of the day, and I can really see an awareness growing in them of noticing what others do for them and with them.

Diagnosis:
Why do you think joy, prayer, and thankfulness are God's will for us as the verse states?

Why are these three things necessary in a homeschool setting? What would a homeschool look like without these traits?

Prescription:
Spend this week focusing on instituting your own rituals and ideas to spark joy, prayer, and thankfulness in your homeschool. Record what you did for each and the result.

Week 8

For this reason, make every effort to supplement your faith with virtue and virtue with knowledge. —2 Peter 1:5

The most frequent question I receive from people who are thinking of homeschooling is what they need to do before they begin. My response usually is surprising to them, because I say, "Make sure that your children listen to you." I never really thought of the biblical principle behind my words until I read the above verse from 2 Peter where Peter says virtue is needed before knowledge. Virtue, or character, is of course, not a one and done proposition when children are involved. It requires constant, diligent training, but if your children are not willing to listen to your instruction when it comes to obedience, kindness, truthfulness, how to treat others, respectfulness, etc., I promise you they will not listen to your instruction about academic matters.

Peter is giving us a key piece of the homeschooling puzzle. Teach your children to have good character, and you can teach them anything. It is not an odd thing to hear other homeschoolers recommend school books be laid aside for a time to address a character issue that has appeared with your children. Charlotte Mason, a British educator from the 1800's whose methods are popular in homeschool circles, devoted entire class periods to habit training in early elementary grades. She knew that to be accomplished in their studies at the higher grades, children would need character or habits that knowledge could be built upon.

In Proverbs 12:1, Solomon drives home this point by saying, "Whoever loves discipline loves knowledge, but he who hates reproof is stupid." Discipline doesn't necessarily mean punishment, but guidance or training. Notice again the order in which these take place. Discipline or training in virtue and character come first, then knowledge can be loved and enjoyed.

Too often as homeschool parents, we feel the burden of academic education, but we must not forget that knowledge can only be truly learned when a foundation of good virtue, character, and habits has been laid.

Diagnosis:
Why would it be difficult to teach someone who hasn't been taught virtue or good character habits?

Are there any virtues or habits that you have become lax about enforcing with your children? Why?

Prescription:
Pull some inspiration from Charlotte Mason and take a habit training sabbatical for a week. Make a list of 2-3 character traits and 1-2 habit routines on which to focus. In the space below, record the things you are working on and how you plan to practice and study those things. You'll be amazed when you pick up your studies next week at how much better knowledge is imparted.

Week 9

Children, obey your parents in the Lord, for this is right...Fathers, do not provoke your children to anger, but bring them up in the discipline and instruction of the Lord.

—Ephesians 6:1, 4

These verses will be used for the next week as well, but for this week the focus will be on verse one. I truly believe that Ephesians 6:1 is the first memory verse most parents have their children learn, for obvious reasons. Especially in homeschooling, it is important that your children listen to you and do what you ask. Whenever education and school lessons enter the mix, obedience, as it pertains to school, becomes more difficult to ascertain. Sometimes our children don't obey because other factors are interfering with their ability to learn, and it's not a case of blatant disobedience.

Make sure what you are asking is age and ability appropriate.
Not too long ago I asked Sophia, my middle child, to copy a sentence in cursive. She'd completed her cursive workbook so of course I knew she was ready to tackle copying a sentence. She's a smart cookie, so I was certain this would be simple. Except it wasn't. She made it through about one word, threw down her pencil in frustration, and said, "I can't do this, Mom!" She was totally right. While she'd learned how to write each individual letter in cursive and had written words here and there, her skills were not ready to tackle a full sentence. I had asked her to do something above her ability level. She was not intending to be disobedient, but was genuinely struggling. Homeschool parents have a tendency to push children before they are ready. Some areas where I've been guilty of this include asking my children to do an assignment they weren't ready to do (as the example above), giving them an assignment that's too easy, trying to push them to be independent with their school work too quickly, and making their time sitting at a desk or table way too lengthy for their age without enough breaks to run and play.

Set them up to succeed.
Almost 90% of the time, disobedience in my children is due to other factors that my children express through bad attitudes. While it seems obvious, when it comes to school time, it is no different. One thing I've discovered this year with my tween is that her sleep needs have gone through the roof. It's like having a toddler again. Many times her unwillingness to even attempt an assignment or a quick frustration level over school work is her way of letting me know she needs some sleep. I can't tell you how many times this past year I sent her to her room to regain control of her emotions that I found her sleeping ten minutes later. She wasn't ready to succeed at school because she was tired. Other things to check if your children are acting squirrelly when it comes to school are hunger, and the need to move. Another way to make sure your children will finish their school work to your satisfaction is to

make sure they have been given explicit instructions of what you want them to do, and supervision. Sometimes you need to make the instructions so detailed it seems ridiculous, but do what you must. I have another child who cannot be sent out of the room to work on anything. Some children need that supervision to stay on task. It's not a big deal for them to stay in the room with me, if it means their work is done well and timely. None of these are disobedience issues, but many times we treat them as such.

Make sure it's not a learning challenge.
While I, as far as I know to this point, don't have a child with a learning disability, I have watched homeschool moms have loads of guilt when they find out the reason their child refused to write wasn't disobedience, but dysgraphia. Or what seemed like daydreaming and not following instructions was actually attention deficit disorder. If you fall in this category, please don't blame yourself for past actions when you didn't know better. If this could possibly be your child, then do whatever you can to get them tested and confirm your suspicions. It's always more helpful when teaching a child to know exactly what you're dealing with than operating from a place of ignorance.

Diagnosis:
Do you find obedience in school work more or less difficult than regular parent and child obedience?

Have there ever been instances where your child didn't obey because your expectations were unrealistic? Because they weren't properly supported with food, sleep, instructions, etc.?

Are there certain situations or assignments where your child always complains or becomes frustrated? This could be a red flag that your child has a learning disability.

Prescription:
Be acutely aware of the assignments and tasks you give your children this week. If disobedience occurs, instead of reacting with discipline, see if your request is appropriate and if you have set them up to succeed, or if this is a regular occurrence with these types of assignments. Take appropriate steps to remedy any of the possibilities causing the behavior before using discipline.

Week 10

Children, obey your parents in the Lord, for this is right...Fathers, do not provoke your children to anger, but bring them up in the discipline and instruction of the Lord.

—Ephesians 6:1, 4

This week I wanted to focus on the second verse. I know it's specifically addressed to fathers, but, honestly, even homeschool moms can be guilty of this admonition.

The day I realized I had been provoking my children to anger and the detriment it was causing our school day was when I read the following on a homeschool forum: when children become emotional, learning stops. That simple sentence rocked me back on my heels. How many times had I witnessed this with my own children?!? They become frustrated with something they are learning. I try, yet again, to explain. They begin to cry, and now I become frustrated. If they'd just be quiet and let me tell them, then they'd understand! My tone becomes sterner as I try to force them to stop their emotional outburst. Now their anger erupts because they feel I'm pushing too hard, but I refuse to let them leave and force them to sit there until I've finished the lesson. I think, "Seriously, child, just sit there and stop your bellyaching so you can finish up. There's no reason to cry or get angry because you don't understand this." There are so many things wrong with the above scenario and it's all summed up with the command to not provoke your children to anger.

Looking back, I readily acknowledge that I was expecting a standard of behavior from them to which I do not even hold myself. When I find myself frustrated in some endeavor, I walk away to give my brain a rest and to calm myself before I attempt it again. However, I constantly find myself forcing my children to stay and tough it out. And for what? They didn't learn anything because I almost always had to reteach the lesson or have them redo the work.

This verse tells us this will always be the case when we push our children past their breaking point. Provoking a child to anger is contrasted with bringing up a child in the discipline and instruction of the Lord by that conjunction "but." In other words, the two cannot happen at the same time. God knows if a child is angry or emotional, they cannot be trained. Do not mistake disobedience for frustration, because if you try to treat frustration as an obedience issue by forcing a child to continue with whatever is frustrating them, you will gain nothing.

Diagnosis:
Have you been guilty of trying to force learning when your children are upset? If so, did it work?

Do you find yourself needing to walk away from things when you are frustrated? Why do you not let your children do so?

Prescription:
Focus on frustration in your children and your response this week. When frustration rears its head, remove whatever is causing problems and set it aside until later. Do a quick brain reset with a snack, some play, or a walk around the block.

Week 11

And she vowed a vow and said, "O Lord of hosts, if you will indeed look on the afflic-tion of your servant and remember me and not forget your servant, but will give to your servant a son, then I will give him to the Lord all the days of his life, and no razor shall touch his head." —1 Samuel 1:11

Before I became a mom, I attended a women's retreat where the speaker had us write down the five most important things in our lives. As she gave her speech, she would randomly ask us to mark off another item on our list and consider it God asking us to give those things up for Him. The one item on the list that most of the women had difficulty removing was their children. Looking back on that exercise now, I understand their hesitation.

The verses above are the words of Hannah dedicating her son to God. She rec-ognized from Whom the blessing of her child came and knew that God loved and would care for Samuel more than she ever could. As homeschool parents, it can be difficult to remember that we must give ultimate control to God.

Give God control of their education.
Yes, you are the teacher. Yes, you are the one who has to get up every day and put on your teacher hat. But often times, I believe we take on too much of the burden. It is not your fault if your child is always a horrible speller despite the fact you use five different spelling programs. It does not make you a bad homeschool mom if your child is a couple of grade levels behind in math because it takes them longer to process and learn. Instead of punishing yourself or your child, give God control of their education. It doesn't mean you quit teaching or quit trying to find solutions to learning problems, but you do stop taking all of that on yourself. God loves your child even more than you do. He will work things out for their education in His own time if you will lean on Him and trust Him to do so.

Give God control of their future.
I remember commenting not too long ago that I'd be happy if my oldest graduated high school by the time she turned twenty. At the time, she was struggling with her current math program, and it seemed we were spinning our wheels instead of mov-ing forward. She wants to attend college, which has minimum requirements in math education, so I was feeling the pressure of time. But then I started thinking, "What does it matter if she goes to college at nineteen or twenty? Maybe that's exactly what needs to happen, or maybe she'll become inspired as high school looms clos-er and she'll do two years of math in one." One thing I did realize was that at some point I can no longer control the parameters of my children's lives. I can't force my children to study or learn. I can't force them to pursue their goals on a specific time table. We must learn now that their future is in God's hands. He knows the plans He

has prepared for them and is in control of them. It's not my place to try and take that control back. God can definitely do a better job of that than I can.

Give God control of their faith.
Out of everything that is difficult to do as Christian parents, this is probably number one. At some point, we need to let our children develop their own faith in the Lord. Hopefully, this happens while they are under your roof. They learn how to study their Bible, how to apply God's word to their own lives, have an active prayer life, and serve others with you encouraging and guiding them. You have a relatively small window of time to impart your faith to your children, and then they must live the rest of their lives with their own faith choices. Thankfully, homeschooling gives us more time with our children to help them develop that faith. The Bible tells us that God wants all people to be saved (1 Timothy 2:3-4), which includes our children. Their faith is in good hands, God's hands, if we are willing to place it there and not carry that burden ourselves.

If God is in control, in what role does that leave us? We are servants, His hands and feet on this earth. Our inadequate and imperfect teaching and mothering abilities are still more than adequate with God leading their lives.

Diagnosis:
Why do you think it is difficult to give our children completely over to God?

Do you find yourself holding on to aspects of your child's education, future, and faith instead of completely trusting God to handle all of it? In what ways do you do this?

How does taking on the role of servant to God's leadership change how you view homeschooling?

Prescription:
Spend time this week praying over your children individually. Pray for God to guide their education, their future, and their faith. You can do this with each child present or do it in private, but make sure to truly give God control and pray for your role as his faithful servant.

Week 12

For this reason I remind you to fan into flame the gift of God, which is in you through the laying on of my hands, for God gave us a spirit not of fear but of power and love and self-control. —2 Timothy 1:6-7 (Sections of these verses will be discussed over the next two weeks. This week we are focusing on the bolded section.)

W hen we first started homeschooling, I was most excited about the individualized education I could provide my children. As a former public school teacher, the thought of being able to choose curriculum, subjects, and teaching methods that were personally tailored to my kids was what I'd dreamed of doing in the classroom. I had no idea, however, just how individualized their educations would be! I have one child who loves math, and another one who thinks it's the worst four letter word in the English language. One child enjoys anything to do with the arts and another would rather build with Legos and play Minecraft. Needless to say, the way their school day looks is definitely varied.

The ability to "fan into flame the gift of God" is something that is uniquely suited to a homeschool setting. As homeschoolers, we are eyewitnesses of our children's varied interests, their inherent strengths, and natural gifts. Let your observations inspire your curriculum choices, subjects studied, and how you present material.

Most importantly, help your children see how they can use those gifts of God to bless the church. Have a math kid? The church always needs accountants. Have a science kid? The church always needs scientists to teach truth. Have an artsy kid? The church always needs people to design bulletin boards, decorate classrooms, and illustrate Bible materials. The sky is the limit with what our children can do for the Lord, but only if we look for those opportunities instead of forcing our children to fit within a specific mold of what a curriculum, neighbors, or relatives say they should be achieving.

Don't let checking boxes off your lesson plans squelch your duty to let your child's God-given gifts burst into flame. It truly is one of our greatest homeschool strengths.

Diagnosis:
Observe your child this week. If you have more than one child, choose a different child to observe on different days. Make notes of their talents, interests, and passions.

Brainstorm a list of ways these gifts could be used in the church.

Prescription:
Make it a point to help each of your children use one of their talents this week to help someone even if it's something small. Record what they did and for whom.

Week 13

*For this reason I remind you to fan into flame the gift of God, **which is in you through the laying on of my hands**, for God gave us a spirit not of fear but of power and love and self-control. —2 Timothy 1:6-7 (A section of this verse was discussed last week and the rest will be discussed next week. This week we are focusing on the bolded section.)*

Obviously this verse is talking about the miraculous ability to lay hands on someone that was used in the first century Christian church to impart miraculous spiritual gifts, but the applications are useful for the homeschool parent as well. When fanning into flame the gift of God in your child, it is a hands-on process. Many of us can probably remember people who encouraged our gifts and talents over the years. By looking at this verse through different eyes, we can see two major points that apply to us as homeschool parents.

1. It takes active participation from us. To help a child find their gift and fan it into flame requires someone to recognize that gift and encourage it. Help them to see the possibilities and dream what could be. You cannot help your child find their gift if you are not involved with their education beyond handing them a checklist of work to complete each day. It will involve time spent with them, engaging with them about what they are studying, and helping them see through a lens for the Lord.

2. It needs to be done through your hands. Since many homeschool parents are products of public or private schools, we generally see teachers and coaches as those who inspire children. However as homeschoolers we have our children with us day in and day out to be their cheerleader, encourager, and dreamer alongside them. Do not neglect this opportunity or, even worse, be a discourager of your child's gifts because they aren't practical or career-oriented.

Our children are in our home to be nurtured and taught by us as we help them realize their full potential as human beings and as Christians. A big part of that is how they will use the gifts God has given them to enrich their lives and the lives of others. We need to make sure our hands are doing the shaping.

Diagnosis:
Do you act interested in your children's passions and interests or relieved that they are occupied?

Are you critical or supportive of your child's endeavors, especially if you don't understand them or enjoy them yourself?

Do you send your children off with books and workbooks to do on their own, or do you make it a point to discuss things they are learning and books they are reading at a deep level so you can better understand them and their thoughts?

What message do you believe your speech and your actions send your children about their interests and their education?

Prescription:
Take a long, honest look at how you respond during the school day when your children pursue their passions and interests. At the end of this week make sure to spend at least 30 minutes with each child and really learn about what excites and inspires them. Make time to engage in that activity with them even if it means they have to teach you! Record what you did with each child and something you learned about your child or their interest.

Week 14

*For this reason I remind you to fan into flame the gift of God, which is in you through the laying on of my hands, **for God gave us a spirit not of fear but of power and love and self-control.** —2 Timothy 1:6-7*

There are numerous fears we have as homeschool parents, and most of those will be discussed in various ways throughout this book, but right now focus on the words that are bolded above and notice four things.

1. Fear does not come from God. If you are afraid, anxious, and worried about educating your children, then you are in a place God doesn't want you to be. There are plenty of moments where you will need to be proactive about researching ideas to overcome an academic struggle or take time to focus on specific character issues that arise, but dwelling and abiding in a place of fear is not how a Christian should live. For homeschool moms, dwelling in fear can ruin your homeschool and your relationship with your children.

2. God gives us power. If there is one thing God possess in abundance, it's power. Power to create universes. Power to raise the dead. Power to save our souls. God has given you use of his power in your homeschool. His power will sustain you when you feel like you can't listen to one more word being sounded out and when you need to try just one more time to explain long division. His power will direct the steps of those in your home down the paths He wishes for you to walk.

3. God gives us love. God is love, and He loves you and your children. He loves you when you lose your temper. He loves you when the house is a mess. He loves you when you crash into bed exhausted every night. Why? Because He loves your children more than you do, and He knows that these children are raised by a mother and father who give up many things to make sure they are educated in a place that honors Him and His word.

4. God gives us self-control. It's hard some days to drag myself out of bed and do the things I know need to be done. It's often too easy to make excuses about why school is not necessary that day, why chores can be put off, or why the kids can park themselves in front of screens for hours on end. But God has given me self-control. While everyone enjoys a day off, it can be very easy to slip into a pattern where self-control is no longer present in my life or the lives of my children. God wants us to be successful and He knows that we will need self-control to do that.

If fear is present, God's gifts cannot function. We must do everything possible to banish fear and soak in the good. A homeschool governed by power, love, and self-control will be a mighty force indeed.

Diagnosis:
What are you most afraid of when you think about homeschooling?

When do you feel the need for God's power the most urgently in your homeschool? His love?

Is a lack of self-control an issue for you? How does it cause difficulties in your homeschool?

Prescription:
Use your Bible's concordance or a digital resource to look up verses about God's power, love, and self-control. Copy a verse about each of these, and place them in an area where you will see them regularly during school time, like your teacher planner or taped somewhere in your school area. Pray over these verses every day with your children before you start your school work. Write down any positive outcomes you noticed in your mood, the school day, your children, etc. Here are some verses to get you started for each one:

Power:
Ephesians 6:10; Zephaniah 3:17; Matthew 19:26; Psalm 28:7; Psalm 147:4-5

Love:
Romans 8:38-39; Ephesians 2:4-5; 1 Peter 5:6-7; Psalm 86:15; Matthew 7:11

Self-Control:
Proverbs 25:28; Galatians 5:22-23; 2 Peter 1:5-7; 1 Corinthians 9:24-27a; Titus 1:8; Romans 12:1-2

Week 15

Therefore I tell you, do not be anxious about your homeschool, what they will learn or what they will not, nor about tests, how well they will score. Is not education more than tests, and knowledge more than what is learned in textbooks? Look at the apostles, they were not greatly educated nor instructed in the learning of their day and yet your heavenly Father used them for his purpose. Are your children not as valuable as they? And which of you mothers by being anxious can change anything about your child's future?

And why are you anxious about your homeschool? Consider your children, how they grow and learn throughout their time at home, yet I tell you, even Solomon in all of his wisdom did not always live as one who was wise. But if God gives you children, which today are in your home and tomorrow are in homes of their own, will he not much more bless them with wisdom and knowledge, O you of little faith?

Therefore do not be anxious saying, 'What if I forget to teach them about the Industrial Revolution?' or 'What if they can't get into college?' or 'What if they work at McDonald's their entire lives?' For people of the world pursue these things, and your heavenly Father knows what your children will need for their futures. But teach your children to seek first the kingdom of God and his righteousness and all the education and knowledge will be added to them. Therefore do not be anxious about your children's futures for the future has enough anxiety for itself. Sufficient for your homeschool is the wisdom of God. —My personal rewrite of Matthew 6:25-34 if Jesus was talking to homeschool mothers

---

Diagnosis:
What worries, doubt, and fears do you have about educating your children?

What does this rewritten passage say is the main thing for your children to learn?

What is His promise if they seek the kingdom first?

If you really believe Jesus' promise as it applies to your children's education, what worries, doubts, and fears should you have?

Prescription:
This week make it a point to teach your children to seek the kingdom. Be specific with how you can do this (Hint: Maybe not stress academics as much and stress God more).

Week 16

Come to me, all who labor and are heavy laden, and I will give you rest. Take my yoke upon you, and learn from me, for I am gentle and lowly in heart, and you will find rest for your souls. For my yoke is easy and my burden is light. —Matthew 11:28-20

When my husband traveled to India a few years ago for mission work, he witnessed this metaphor in real life. He saw water buffalo with huge, heavy wooden yokes on their necks. They were so heavy that they actually pushed down into their skin. It had to be very uncomfortable for those animals!

As Christians who have chosen to homeschool, we feel the extra burden, the heavy yoke, of having the sole responsibility for our child's academic success. We labor day in and day out to make sure our children achieve certain standards in reading, math, writing, etc., and it is exhausting!

But notice that Jesus contrasts His yoke to the heavy wooden yoke of the oxen. Jesus describes His yoke as easy and light. He says that when we wear His yoke, we will find rest for our souls. Doesn't this sound like a wonderful way to describe our homeschool: easy, light, and rest?

There is no doubt that every homeschool has "heavy yoke" days. Just like our Christian walk, we will never achieve perfection this side of heaven, but our homeschool should have the general tenure of easy, light, and rest. So why do we so consistently fall into the trap of carrying a heavy load through our homeschool days?

Let's apply Jesus' metaphor of yokes to homeschooling:

Our Homeschool Labor	
Heavy Yoke	**Easy Yoke**
1. Find stress	1. Find rest
2. An overwhelming burden	2. A light burden
3. Feel loaded down	3. Feel at peace
4. Learn from the world	4. Learn from Jesus
(selfish and succeed at any cost)	(gentleness and lowly in heart)

The difference in each yoke you carry depends upon who placed it there, Jesus or the world.

Diagnosis:
What words would you use to describe the yoke of your homeschool (rushed, stressful, relaxed, engaging, etc.)?

Compare the words you used to the words Jesus uses to describe His yoke (rest, gentle, easy, light).

How have you let the world's yoke influence your homeschool? In what ways?

Prescription:
Pinpoint the number one thing that makes your homeschool day feel like a heavy yoke. Spend tomorrow coming up with a game plan to target that stressor. Ask your children to help you brainstorm creative ideas to help solve the problem. Most likely, if it stresses you out, it stresses them out as well. Here are some examples of things that caused stress in our homeschool that I changed: teaching both science and history during the week, combining my children for subjects, and not getting enough sleep. In the space below, write your stressor and the solutions you brainstormed. Give one of the solutions a try out this week, and at the end of the week, write your assessment of how it went. Talk it over with your children and see if you need to adjust that solution or try one of your other solutions.

Week 17

For the body does not consist of one member but of many. If the foot should say, "Because I am not a hand, I do not belong to the body," that would not make it any less a part of the body. And if the ear should say, "Because I am not an eye, I do not belong to the body," that would not make it any less a part of the body. If the whole body were an eye, where would be the sense of hearing? If the whole body were an ear, where would be the sense of smell? But as it is, God arranged the members in the body, each one of them, as he chose. If all were a single member, where would the body be? As it is, there are many parts, yet one body. —1 Corinthians 12: 14-20

I love homeschooling in the modern technological age. The internet has made it easier than ever for homeschoolers to make connections with each other to the benefit of all. Homeschoolers are, on the whole, more than happy to share curriculum ideas, solutions to problems, free resources, and encouragement. Too often, though, homeschooling in the tech age has a dark side: the comparison trap. Because homeschoolers are so eager to share via blogs, social media, and online communities, it is very easy to feel that your own homeschool is inadequate or lacking in some way.

Just like the church is made up of many members with different functions and gifts, the homeschooling community is also made up of many different types of philosophies and families. No two homeschools should look alike. We are each blessed with different personalities, learning styles, family culture, beliefs, socio-economic levels, and a thousand other differences. If you are constantly chasing after another family's homeschool, you are bound to fail. You must find what methods, curriculums, and routines work for your home.

Ultimately, finding your niche in the homeschool world boils down to two things: choice and confidence. Make your choices about curriculum and/or learning philosophy, and teach with confidence. For some of us this is easier said than done! It is difficult to walk the tight rope of searching blogs for ideas and inspiration, reading homeschool forums for help with a specific issue, and building Pinterest boards of awesome projects and experiments without falling off into jealousy, covetousness, and discouragement.

Continue to peek into the lives of various homeschool families, but know that just because their family participates in the Renaissance Fair doesn't mean your family should as well. Use the ideas that work and forget about ones that don't. There is no right way to homeschool. One type of homeschool is not more valid than another. It takes all of us to weave this beautiful tapestry of homeschooling, so don't let other homeschools make you feel like a failure or an overachiever. If your family is building strong relationships, if your children are learning, if God is your rock, you are succeeding. Differences are good and necessary.

Diagnosis:
How is your family different from other homeschool families you know or interact with online? Ex: reasons for homeschooling, scheduling, curriculum, educational philosophy, etc.

How is your family similar to other homeschool families you know or interact with online?

Prescription:
Celebrate your uniqueness! List below all the ways homeschooling is perfect for your family and all the ways you've adapted homeschooling to your family culture. There is no other family out there quite like yours, so be proud of that fact, not fearful.

Week 18

But with me it is a very small thing that I should be judged by you or by any human court. In fact, I do not even judge myself. For I am not aware of anything against myself, but I am not thereby acquitted. It is the Lord who judges me.

—1 Corinthians 4:3-4

Oh, if only I could agree with Paul that it is a small thing to be judged by others! If you've been homeschooling for any amount of time, you've most likely been on the receiving end of some negative comments about your choice to homeschool. Those comments might come from friends and family, from total strangers, or even from your own negative self-talk. The beauty of this passage is that our homeschool is not judged by others. Our homeschool is not judged by our own standards for success. Our homeschool is judged only by the Lord and his standards. Let's look at some ways we displease and please God in our homeschool.

How Not to Please God (Mark 8:36)
Focus on academics more than relationships. When you homeschool, it is very easy to fall into the trap of focusing on the "school" part more than the "home" part. It is perfectly understandable that we do this since our children's academic success is much more measureable and admired than the strength of their bond with parents, siblings, and God. Don't be tempted by the praise of men; God is pleased by developing strong loving relationships in families and with Him.

Not educate your children. While solely prioritizing academics is bad, solely prioritizing "spiritual" endeavors over academics is equally displeasing. When you commit to homeschooling, you are agreeing to educate your child in compliance with your state laws. While methods, curriculum, and other variables may come into play, allowing our children to not be educated is displeasing to God because Christians are to follow the laws of the land (Romans 13:1-7).

Make homeschooling an idol. To be honest, this is a trap that Christian homeschool moms can fall into without even realizing it. Our motives are pure; we want our children to grow up and become Christians. However, to achieve that goal, we set out to control everything we can that will give them an advantage to keep the faith. This isn't wrong, but many times homeschooling becomes what we depend on to "save" our children. God is not pleased with this view. There is only one Savior of our children, His Son.

How to Please God (Matthew 22:36-40)
Use your time to point your children to Him. As homeschoolers we have the unique opportunity to make every lesson, every subject, and every discussion God-centered. You can purchase curriculum to help you or you can inject your own Biblical lessons

during the day. All of this provides a constant focus on God and an awareness of Him throughout all subjects that extend beyond Bible lessons and Bible class at church. God is always pleased when we lead others to a deeper knowledge of Him.

Use your time to serve others. To be honest, I'd never thought about homeschooling being the perfect vehicle for service until last year when a speaker at a homeschool conference was talking about all the ways she and her children serve their community and church as part of their homeschool. It made me realize how pleasing it is to God when we use our days to serve others and love our neighbors as ourselves.

Use your time to strengthen your family. Too often I find myself checking out mentally and emotionally once the school day is done, but I know that staying engaged is definitely pleasing to the Lord. Creating strong family bonds and a strong family culture centered on God is what He desires for all families, and homeschoolers are no different. The difference is that we are around each other 24/7 which can cause the opposite response if we aren't careful, so we must be diligent to create opportunities daily and weekly for everyone to reconnect as a family.

Diagnosis:
Do you feel you are pleasing or displeasing God in your homeschool? Why?

What changes could you make to please him more?

Prescription:
Create a list of ideas for each of the God-pleasing categories that you can implement right away. How can I point my children even more to God during our day (time set aside for God-focused discussions, memorization of scripture, etc.)? How can I find ways to serve others with my children during our homeschool week (delivering food to those in need, canned food drive, etc.)? How can our family carve out special time each day to just be a family together (special routines or family nights, etc.)? Start these habits in your home and homeschool this week.

Week 19

He said, "The Lord is my rock and my fortress and my deliverer, my God, my rock in whom I take refuge, my shield, and the horn of my salvation, my stronghold and my refuge, my savior; you save me from violence. —2 Samuel 22:2-3

When I was an education major about sixteen years ago, one of the required classes was Educational Psychology. Basically the class was to teach us how the brain works when it comes to learning. One of the theories we learned about was Maslow's Hierarchy of Needs. Maslow's theory as applied to education is that children cannot learn unless they have certain needs met that enable them to be able to receive the instruction you are providing. The lowest level of needs is survival needs: food, water, clothing, shelter, etc. The next level is the one on which I want to focus: security or safety.

Your first thought might be, "Of course my children are safe and secure in our home," and I have no doubt they are. But do they feel safe in regards to you as their teacher? Ask yourself if you have ever done any of the following:

- When your child forgets a concept that you've taught multiple times, do you mention all the previous times you've already gone over it in an exasperated voice?
- Do you get frustrated and short with your kids when they struggle with something that should be simple?
- Do you yell and get angry at your children to make them hurry and finish their school work?

We've all been there, but if this seems to be the default mode in your homeschool, I can guarantee you, they don't feel safe. They may placate you and fake it, but they know that safety is only an illusion until mom gets upset again.

Your children need to feel safe with you to learn. Otherwise they will be so worried about disappointing you or angering you that they cannot give their full attention to what you are teaching. In full disclosure, a lack of safety in our homeschool, which was completely my fault as outlined above, characterized my children's education for far too long. Only in the past couple of years have I made a concerted effort to change because I could see the damage it was doing to my children and their relationship with me. I wanted my children to be able to read the verses above from 2 Samuel and replace "Mom" for "God." Do your children feel safe enough in your homeschool to say those verses about you?

My children say, "My mom is my rock and my fortress and my deliverer, my mom, my rock in whom I take refuge, my shield, and the horn of my salvation, my stronghold and my refuge, my savior; you save me from violence."

Diagnosis:
Have you as a homeschool teacher made your children feel unsafe? How?

Why do you believe you find yourself responding with frustration, anger, or exasperation when your children struggle? (Hint: It's usually based in fear of something).

Prescription:
The moment I realized that something needed to change in our homeschool was when I was perusing the internet and I came across a statement. I'm sure I'm not quoting it exactly, nor do I know where I originally read it, but it was similar to this: The way you respond when your child struggles with a math problem is the way they perceive God responds when they struggle with sin in their lives. Wow. From that moment on, I knew I needed to work on safety and security in our homeschool. Here's the steps I went through (and I still work through!) when I realized what kind of atmosphere I'd been creating. These steps are also your challenge this week.

Step 1: Apologize to your children and ask for their forgiveness. You have wronged them, and you need to let them know you recognize that.

Step 2: Create a code word or signal for both the children and you to use when frustration, anger, or exasperation is close to the surface. You can choose something funny like "pickle snot" to say or something more traditional like "time out," but whatever you choose, the signal lets mom and children know that someone needs to take a few minutes to compose themselves.

Step 3: Chart your progress. Find some way to record how all of you do with controlling frustration and anger, a calendar, a sticker chart, etc. This is such an encouraging way to watch yourself break a bad habit.

Step 4: Work on rebuilding relationships. When your children don't feel safe, they don't want to spend time with you or share with you. Seek each of your children out for some one-on-one time outside of school hours every day. Talk to them, play with them, exercise with them or anything else that interests them, but do something every day to reconnect as parent and child.

Week 20

There is no fear in love, but perfect love casts out fear. For fear has to do with punishment, and whoever fears has not been perfected in love. —1 John 4:18

Last week we focused on making sure our children feel safe, but if we are going to really sustain a secure and loving learning environment for our children, we need to look at why we become frustrated, angry, exasperated, and short-tempered during school time.

There are a variety of reasons for our negative emotions to bubble to the surface, from being hungry or tired, to unloading our stress or anger at other situations and people onto our children. However, I suspect that a large part of the lack of safety in our homes comes from fear.

Homeschooling is a frightening proposition due to being the person solely responsible for your child's education. The antidote to fear is given in the verse above: love. When you are a homeschool mom, you need to direct this love toward three recipients.

Children: Most likely you began homeschooling out of love for your children, putting their best interests first, either academically, spiritually, socially, or some combination of all three. When fear begins to creep in, remember why you started this journey: love for your children. Focus on that and not fear. Don't hurt your relationship because you're afraid.

Ourselves: Do you love yourself? Do you show that love by taking time to do things just for you? Many times as homeschool moms, we don't have time to do anything for ourselves once our mother, household, and homeschool duties are completed for the day. Sometimes this lack of self-care manifests as anger and frustration because we're exhausted and on empty.

God: As Christians, our entire faith is centered around God's love for us and our love for God. However, I often catch myself saying I love God, but living my life as if I don't trust Him. It's not really love if I doubt God. God has promised in Isaiah 41:13, "For I, the Lord your God, hold your right hand; it is I who say to you, 'Fear not, I am the one who helps you.'" The closer we are to God and the more we love Him, the easier it is to trust His promises.

Diagnosis:
How did love for your children lead you to homeschooling?

What are some ways you show love to yourself each day?

If we truly love and trust God, how should that combat the fear we feel as we homeschool?

Prescription:
This week your challenge is all about love!

1. Plan one day this week to do nothing, but love on your kids (go on a picnic, movies, bike riding, etc.), whatever your children love to do with you.

2. Choose a different day this week to show some love to you (coffee shop, library/bookstore, massage, manicure, gym, etc.).

3. Shower some love on God, who He is, what He's done, promises He's kept and will keep. Write a letter to Him one day this week or over several days.

Week 21

Whatever you do, work heartily as for the Lord and not for men. —Colossians 3:23

Diligence. It's probably my number one consistent struggle in my years of homeschooling. When the children were younger, diligence with school was not really necessary. A day's worth of school could be completed in an hour or a little more. It wasn't uncommon for us to only do school for a couple of days each week. To be perfectly honest, it was because I wouldn't be in the mood to do so, not because of illness, life changes, or any other valid reason. I would much rather have been reading, watching TV, or clicking around on the internet, so I did. Plus I couldn't really see any detriment to my lackadaisical attitude. The girls learned to read, stayed on grade level with math and writing, and we dabbled in history and science. What I didn't know is I had sowed seeds that would yield a crop of laziness and bad attitudes.

A few years ago, with my oldest quickly approaching the middle grades and my youngest joining our school routine soon, I realized now was the time to buckle down and get serious about our school work. Not a heavy-handed approach, but consistency. Imagine my surprise when my children balked. My lack of diligence had created children who weren't diligent in school either. The days and months of teaching and training this character trait were not enjoyable for anyone involved, including myself.

If only I'd thought about the above verse all those years ago. The work of educating my children was not done heartily, nor was it done as if I was doing it for the Lord. It was definitely all about me and what I wanted to do those days, including not dealing with children who were resistant because they wanted to veg in front of the TV instead of learn. I didn't really believe it mattered. No one could see what was happening in our home, but God could see. He could see me choosing self over service and letting my children choose laziness over education. Not a pretty sight for sure!

I share this cautionary tale with you so you can learn a few lessons from my mistakes:

1. If you aren't diligent, most likely your children will not be either. A classic case of "do what I say and not what I do": it's well and good to tell your children they need to complete some school work, when mom lazed around all morning in bed or on the couch. I don't think your words are matching the reality. To be honest, I don't blame the kids. It really isn't fair to be asked to do something your parental example isn't willing to do.

2. Sometimes we are diligent in some areas, but not in others. I discovered this little nugget of truth when I started trying to turn things around in our homeschool. It wasn't difficult to be diligent about math (I knew they needed it), language arts (I am comfortable teaching this area), Bible (obviously necessary), and history (my true love), but when it came to being diligent with science (ugh), chores (which I hate) or going to bed on time (which I hate even more) so we could all wake up early-ish (which I hate the most), I was not diligent at all. This was a good lesson for all of us in doing what must be done even when it's not fun. "Heartily for the Lord" was my mantra!

3. Diligence doesn't mean strict or harsh. Once you decide to be diligent, it's really easy to come down on everyone with the force of Thor's hammer. In case you are curious, this is not a good approach. When you decide to be more diligent about anything in your home or school, it's best to ease into it so that everyone (including you!) can adjust. Choose to be diligent about one thing for a week. Slowly add more things as the weeks go by until diligence is your new normal, and try to make it a fun and relaxed atmosphere. Change is difficult for everyone, but more so if you don't have a sense of humor and grace as problems arise.

Diagnosis:
In what ways have you not been diligent in your homeschool?

Do you see your lack of diligence as causing problems with your children's diligence?

How does knowing your home education should always be done for the Lord inspire you to practice diligence in your home school?

Prescription:
In whatever areas you or your children haven't been practicing diligence, this is the week to begin a change! Create a competition this week on who can work for the Lord the most consistently. Keep track with a sticker chart or tally marks under each person's name. At the end of the week reward yourselves with something fun, and, of course, keep it going in coming weeks until you all have new habits.

Week 22

Do not be anxious about anything, but in everything by prayer and supplication with thanksgiving let your requests be made known to God. And the peace of God, which surpasses all understanding, will guard your hearts and your minds in Christ Jesus.

—Philippians 4:6-7

Peace. We want it in our world, our lives, and definitely in our homeschools. Peace seems as fleeting as a breath most days in our homeschool. It comes and goes throughout the day, and some days it doesn't put in an appearance at all! But peace is not to be elusive to Christians. It is to be present at all times guarding our hearts and minds.

It's very easy to say this or read it in the Bible, but extremely difficult to do with babies crying, toddlers destroying, children being stubborn, and teens exhibiting raging hormones all while trying to educate everyone and maintain peace in your heart and mind— peace that isn't dependent upon circumstances, but constantly present.

Do not be anxious about anything.

The source of our lack of peace is our own anxiety. It's easy to become anxious when homeschooling. Anxious because the baby was fussy and you couldn't finish your lesson with your third grader. Anxious because your child is just not grasping a concept, so you don't know if you should move forward or not. Anxious because the house seems that it is never clean. Homeschooling brings so many more avenues for anxiety into our lives. However, this anxiety is a peace destroyer, and God knows this, thus His command to not be anxious about anything. No anxiety about your children's education. No anxiety about fussy babies. No anxiety about messy houses. What he's telling us is, "Stop being anxious! I'm in control. Do you really believe that, homeschool mom?"

But in everything by prayer and supplication with thanksgiving let your requests be made known to God.

To cure our anxiety and bring peace into our lives, God asks us to do one thing, pray. Ask Him for help and strength. Have you ever prayed about your homeschool and about situations that cause you to become anxious or stressed? It seems that some days I'm taking a prayer break every thirty minutes to reset my peace. In my opinion, though, the most important part of this equation is that our prayers should be accompanied with thanksgiving. Most days it's difficult to feel thankful about whatever is causing you to be anxious. It definitely requires a change in perception: being thankful for a fussy baby because God has blessed you with this child and you know it's just a season in life, being thankful for a struggling child because they can learn at their own pace without feeling pressure to meet an arbitrary standard, and being thankful that God blessed you with shelter and possessions to create a messy house. Becoming thankful about what is making you anxious is probably the reaction that has brought the biggest peace in my homeschool.

And the peace of God, which surpasses all understanding, will guard your hearts and minds in Christ Jesus.
The end result of stopping our anxiety and bringing our requests to God with thanksgiving is a peace that we can't even understand and a peace that will protect our hearts and minds from further anxiety. Doesn't that sound like a wonderful way to run your homeschool? Before you know it, your response of prayer and thanksgiving becomes a natural reaction to stress in your homeschool that will bleed over into other areas of your life as well.

Diagnosis:
Have you struggled with having peaceful days in your homeschool?

What situations seem to be the triggers for anxiety and stress when it comes to homeschooling?

Do you pray about your homeschool throughout your homeschool day? Why do you think prayer is not our first correctional method we try when things seem to go wrong?

Prescription:
Focus this week on reacting to stress and anxiety with prayer and thanksgiving. It might be helpful to put a picture of praying hands on the school table as a visual reminder of your intended response. Don't forget to help your children learn to react in this way as well because they become stressed and anxious about school as well. Record how it helps you to manage your reactions and stress level below.

Week 23

Look carefully then how you walk, not as unwise but as wise, making the best use of the time, because the days are evil. —Ephesians 5:15-16

Homeschoolers are all given the same twenty-four hours to educate our children. However, all of us could take some scheduling advice from the above verses. We need to be wise with our scheduling so that we are making the best use of our time.

Schedule the most important first.

We all know how easily a day can be thrown off track by life intruding into our school time: sick kids, appointments, emergencies, etc. The possibilities of interruptions are endless. To make sure we cover the necessary, schedule those first. Usually for most families, these are the 4 R's as I like to call them: reading, writing, arithmetic, and religion. By scheduling these first, you have covered the basics and Bible study. I feel that if I can get these accomplished in our day, then I've done a good job educating the children that day. It relieves the burden of feeling guilty if the rest of the day falls apart because I know they have learned the most important subjects already.

Schedule realistically.

There is nothing I like better than to make some beautiful homeschool schedules, color-coded schedules for our day, timed schedules for our week, and precise schedules for our year. They are truly my own personal, geeky works of art. The problem is that I find myself scheduling for perfect days instead of realistic ones. I have every second of our school time scheduled assuming that the children move seamlessly from one subject to another and no need for 30 minute long bathroom breaks in between. While I still love having my schedules, I've learned to be realistic about my children, myself, and how time works in reality. If my schedule says that our entire school day should take about four hours, I need to add an extra hour or hour and a half to that time because that is realistically how it will work out. Is that amount of time going to fit into our day, or do I need to cut some subjects to keep our school day at the four hours I had planned? If you don't make sure your schedule is realistic, it will be frustrating to you and your children trying to work within a schedule that is not flexible.

Schedule for a restful homeschool.

While making sure to cover all of our bases academically is important, it is equally, and possibly more important, to make sure that you have restfulness planned into your day. I'm not necessarily talking about a nap time, but to prioritize not filling the day full of academic pursuits. Give your children the gift of being able to rest and relax and pursue their own interests during your school day. One way I've tried to do this is to give my children a couple of hours every afternoon to play outside, paint, draw, build, play games, read, etc. Nothing electronic involved, of course, because I want them to focus on being together and having fun. This time of day has truly become something we all look forward to because it's my time to relax and rest as well!

When you schedule to make the best use of your time, it requires that you consciously think about what you want your school days to look like. Most of us wouldn't say that we want rushed, hurried, stressed days where we feel stretched thin and collapse in bed at night disappointed that we didn't finish two subjects in our lesson plan. If we take some time to change the way we schedule, we can leave those feelings behind and enjoy our homeschool days.

Diagnosis:
What would you say are the most important subjects to cover each day in your homeschool?

Do you have a problem with overscheduling your days and trying to fit everything into exact time slots? Why do you think we schedule exactly three hours of work and then become shocked or frustrated that it takes longer than that?

Do you have a rest and relax time built into your homeschool day? Why or why not?

Prescription:
Take your current homeschool schedule or routine and examine it through the eye of making the most of your time. Are your priority subjects scheduled first in your day so that they are certain to be completed? Have you given yourself a nice hour to hour and a half cushion in your homeschool day to realistically get everything completed? Do you have some sort of down time planned for you and your children each day? Whatever you need to adjust in your schedule, do so to fit these ideas into your day. Try out your new schedule this week and see how it goes. You can always go back to your old schedule or continue to rearrange things until you find that sweet spot.

Week 24

Hear, O Israel: the Lord our God, the Lord is one. You shall love the Lord your God with all your heart, and with all your soul, and with all your might. And these words that I command to you today shall be on your heart. You shall teach them diligently to your children, and shall talk of them when you sit in your house, and when you walk by the way, and when you lie down, and when you rise. —Deuteronomy 6:6-7

No matter why you initially began homeschooling, the number one benefit to a Christian homeschool family is the ability to live out what these verses say. While all Christian families are charged with this command, homeschoolers have the blessing of time.

Time to teach the Word.
As homeschoolers, you don't lose eight or more hours of the day to the public school system when it comes to teaching your children the word of God. In fact, homeschoolers can infuse all subjects with biblical teaching if they choose. Along with a dedicated Bible program, you can add religious instruction to science, government, history, economics, art, music, and more. I know of one family who taught history from Ancient Mesopotamia through Ancient Rome using nothing but the Bible and the Hebrew nation as their outline and adding supplemental books here and there over various topics. When you permeate your homeschool with God's word, you are giving your children an education in more than just the required subjects. You are diligently teaching the Bible and all of its truths.

Time to memorize the Word.
One of the areas in which I really feel that I slacked off during my oldest daughter's early elementary school years was memorization, especially memorizing scripture. She hated to memorize anything, so I didn't really push it with her, and I was never sure what I should have her memorize. I don't like to go into situations without some kind of plan, and planning our Bible memory work was no different. Once I decided that scripture memorization was a priority, I discovered that planning the verses or passages we would memorize was super helpful. Also, we try to make memorization fun by singing the verses or by adding hand movements to remember the words or phrases. Last year we spent the entire year memorizing passages and chapters from the Psalms. By using your time to memorize, you are putting God's Word on your heart and your children's hearts.

Time to train in the Word.
It's not beneficial to teach and memorize if you don't train your children in the Word. All day long, throughout various conflicts, meltdowns, stubbornness, joys, and sorrows, you can bring your children again and again to God's Word for answers, comfort, and examples of correct and incorrect behavior. We all know that repetition is how

everyone learns best and retains information the longest in our brains. Being able to repeatedly draw our children into the Bible to train them how to be godly citizens and how to be Christians is priceless and a blessing, considering that having children in other school settings just doesn't allow this kind of training due to restraints placed upon teachers by law. You are able to talk about these biblical precepts with your children when you sit, when you walk, when you lie down, and when you rise.

A common saying about motherhood is the days are long, but the years are short. As Christian homeschool moms, we need to make sure we don't fall into the trap of thinking we have plenty of time to teach our children about God's Word. As homeschoolers, God has blessed us with the gift of time; don't waste it.

Diagnosis:
How has homeschooling provided you more time with your children?

What ways do you take advantage of the time you have to live out the commands of the verses above?

Prescription:
Brainstorm all the ways that the Bible is used throughout the day. Is it used in other subjects than Bible study? Do you have Bible study time as a group? Do your children have personal Bible study? Do you make memorization part of your homeschool? Do you have a plan for your memorization? Do you turn to the Bible to guide your homeschool and family? Do you do this in front of your children? After answering these questions, look for any deficiencies in using your time for the Word. Make a plan to address different areas of weaving Bible into your subjects (you don't necessarily need to buy new curriculum), Bible study, scripture memorization, and using the Bible in daily life.

Week 25

How can a young man keep his way pure? By guarding it according to your Word. With my whole heart I seek you; let me now wander from your commandments! I have stored up your Word in my heart, that I might not sin against you.... I will delight in your statutes; I will not forget your Word. —Psalm 119:9-11, 16

I am assuming some things about you and your family this week: 1) you are a Christian, and 2) you want your children to be as well. This passage of scripture, and indeed all of Psalm 119, is about having a deep love for God's Word, a love that leads to obedience and purity in our lives. While fabulous Bible classes and an awesome youth group are helpful, for our children to love God's Word and let it guide their lives, they need to be immersed in scripture as much as possible.

If we are Christian homeschool moms, beyond academics, beyond social opportunities, we need to create homeschools that love God's Word. Here are some suggestions:

Don't use it as punishment. When I was about four years old, my babysitter made a sandwich for me for lunch. She put mayonnaise on it, which I hated. I preferred mustard, but she hadn't asked. When I refused to eat the sandwich, she forced me to eat it anyway. When I finished choking it down, I went in the bathroom and threw up. It took me well into adulthood to be able to tolerate mayonnaise on anything. Don't treat God's Word like mayonnaise with your children. Forcing children to copy scripture as punishment or quoting scripture to them every time they disobey will only result in children who feel the Word is being forced on them before they've learned to love it.

Use it as your guide to life. When your children see you turning to the Bible for guidance and comfort as problems arise, they will learn to turn to it for guidance as well. When they see you making time for Bible study, they will as well. When they see you loving scripture, they will want to love what you love. The best way to help your children love the Word is to model that love for them and share that love with them.

Make memorizing it your first priority. One of the key phrases in the verses above is that storing up God's Word in our hearts helps us to not sin. If memorizing Bible verses has always been something you tried to fit into your schedule when you could, then you are missing one of the most necessary components in Christian homeschooling. When Jesus is tempted in the desert by Satan, he quotes scripture in response to Satan's requests. If knowing God's Word was Jesus' defense, how much more so do our children need recall of biblical truths?

Diagnosis:
Why do you want your children to love the Bible?

Have you been as diligent with creating a love relationship between God's Word and your children as you have with math and reading instruction? Why or why not?

Do you show your love for scripture to your children? How?

Prescription:
Think of practical ways to encourage love of God's Word and implement them this week. Some ideas to get you started:

● Begin a memorization program (the Beatitudes, Psalm 23, or the Lord's Prayer are easy places to start).
● Spend time in Bible study first thing every day with your children (the S.O.A.P method is easy for kids to learn).
● Brainstorm with your kids reasons the Bible is a book we should love.
● When watching cartoons or family movies, use scripture to come up with solutions to the problems the characters encounter (this is a great way for kids to see biblical application in action!).

Now you try to think of some others as well:

Week 26

For freedom Christ has set us free; stand firm therefore, and do not submit again to a yoke of slavery. —Galatians 5:1

This week and the next two weeks will be about our homeschool curriculum and how it can sometimes cause problems in our homeschools.

So many times curriculum can feel like a yoke of slavery. It presses down on us, forcing us to follow the instructions inside. For many years I suffered under the yoke of curriculum slavery. I didn't feel confident enough to try educating on my own. While I still use curriculum for almost all of our subjects, I've learned a couple of lessons about not submitting again to curriculum slavery.

Use Curriculum as a Tool

Many times curriculum is like a warm blanket. You can wrap yourself in it and know that all is right with your homeschool world. You feel safe and secure because all you have to do is teach the curriculum, and your children will be educated. It's homeschool magic. Until the day the fairy tale ends, and you realize that the curriculum you've chosen isn't doing the magical job it's supposed to do. Your child cries when you pull if off the shelf. It stresses you out to teach it. The instructions that it gives seem like a waste of time (Do you really need to rewrite an entire sentence just to underline the subject and circle the predicate?). At this point you feel duped and upset. Why isn't this curriculum working? Most likely you need to recognize that curriculum is an inanimate object. It cannot MAKE you teach any certain way. Probably the most difficult lesson to learn for most homeschool moms is that curriculum, many times, needs to be tweaked to fit your child and your homeschool.

Here are some examples of using curriculum like a tool: The workbook has 30 sentences to diagram. I know that my child can demonstrate mastery if she can diagram six of them, so that's all I assign. We come to a chapter in the math book, and I'm certain my child already knows the information, so I let her take the chapter test and skip the entire chapter. Instead of writing out sentences in the literature guide to answer the questions, I ask the questions orally to my child and have her respond. Turn review time into a game instead of pen and pencil work; review math facts by having them hopscotch to the correct answer; work on spelling by tossing a ball back and forth for each letter in the word; practice phonics sounds by shooting the correct letters with a water gun. In other words, take curriculum and make it into something reflective of you.

Use Curriculum on Your Time Table

My personal struggle with curriculum is the feeling that it has to be completed as the curriculum dictated. If the curriculum was written to be finished in thirty-six weeks, I was determined to make that happen. Obviously my comfortable, warm, secure curriculum knew this was what my child needed. Feeling the crunch of time has a peculiar effect upon most people, including homeschool moms. Imagine this scene: it's Sunday morning, and you are trying to get everyone, including yourself, dressed and fed before leaving home for worship services. No matter how well you plan, it seems something goes wrong every week. There are missing shoes, a diaper that needs changed, a spilled glass of milk, etc. Before you know it, you have fifteen minutes until services start and two children without their hair brushed yet. Once you feel time slipping away from you, the switch is flipped and panicked, anxious mom appears, yelling encouraging words to everyone that quickly moves on to threatening words as she ushers everyone out the door.

Unfortunately, this scene is not one I need to imagine! Curriculum can do the same thing to a homeschool mom. It makes you feel that time crunch and suddenly encouraging mom turns into threatening angry moms. "You are already behind in math and now you haven't finished your work for today!" "Come on! We've still got to finish science today." "Could you please write a little more quickly? You still have five more subjects to do and at this rate, you won't be finished until bedtime!"

Don't give curriculum this power to change your temperament. All that it succeeds in doing is destroying the peace in your homeschool with little being accomplished. I promise you that if you take two days to do a math lesson, your child will still graduate. If you don't finish your curriculum in thirty-six weeks, it doesn't mean you are behind if you continue that curriculum into the next year. No one will show up at your house, drag you into the street and proclaim, "Here is a homeschool mom who took 48 weeks to complete her curriculum. Please come out and throw tomatoes at her as we put her in the stocks." It's your homeschool, and no one but you can determine how long it takes your child to learn and work through the curriculum you've chosen. Don't let your curriculum enslave you.

Diagnosis:
Does curriculum ever feel like a yoke of slavery to you? Why?

Why do you think we let curriculum have so much control in our homeschool instead of recognizing it for the tool it is?

Prescription:
This week, use your curriculum in a purposefully different way. For every subject this week, try to manipulate the curriculum in some way (shortening the length of work, speaking instead of writing, games instead of normal review, acting out a story instead of asking your children to tell you what you read or doing reading comprehension sheets, type their spelling test on the computer, etc.). This doesn't need to be anything fancy because we're working on training you to think outside the box when it comes to curriculum.

But test everything: hold fast what is good. —1 Thessalonians 5:21

Last week, this week, and next week are all about our homeschool curriculum and how it can sometimes cause problems in our homeschools.

One of the first pieces of advice you probably received from other homeschoolers was to determine your homeschool style or methodology. While it can be helpful to research and take quizzes about Charlotte Mason, classical, unschooling, Waldorf, traditional, interest-led, and everything else, labeling yourself and your homeschool can sometimes feel oppressive too. When you classify your educational methods, the verse above is wise counsel to follow.

Test Everything

One of the most recent bits of homeschool wisdom I've adopted was from a talk given by Dr. Christopher Perrin, a classical educator. He said that teachers should make sure principles support practices. In other words, what you do in your homeschool should be an expression of what is important to you. However, if we get too caught up in homeschool methods, it's easy to find ourselves more concerned with doing what the philosophy says instead of analyzing or testing whether that practice is best for our homeschool or our child.

The homeschool style I agree with the most is Charlotte Mason, so about a year ago, I decided to really go full Charlotte Mason and attempt to do everything just like she did in her British schools. We were doing pretty well until we got to Plutarch. In Charlotte Mason's school, students would read from Plutarch's Lives as a citizenship/government type class. I purchased a kid friendly version of Plutarch and we dived in. At first, it wasn't so bad. The story of Brutus, of Julius Caesar fame, was quite riveting and brought up good discussions. However, as we went through more chapters, it became the most dreaded book in our day. I continued to push on because I was trying to be a really good Charlotte Mason homeschool mom. Finally, I couldn't do it anymore. I decided I would use other resources to teach my children about citizenship and government, but it wouldn't be Plutarch no matter how much Ms. Mason found it useful in her schools. Plutarch didn't pass my test of what was best for our homeschool.

Hold Fast to What is Good

I can honestly say I've found bits from all the popular homeschool philosophies to use in our home. From classical, the emphasis on diving deep into subjects instead of skimming. From Socratic, questioning to assess learning. From unschooling, I've gained the reassurance that my children can and will learn what they need. From interest-led learning, I like the reminder that the beauty of homeschooling is my children's ability to learn according to their interests. From Waldorf education, I can focus on ritual and beauty that has added so much to our day. There are also tenants I disagree with in all homeschool philosophies.

Ultimately, you must choose for yourself when it comes to the method or methods you use in your home. Study and learn about each of them. Take away and implement the ideas that fit with your homeschool, and let the rest of it go. Many times, homeschoolers try to put themselves in boxes of their own making instead of realizing there are many options and they do not have to be married to one to call themselves homeschoolers.

Diagnosis:
What homeschool method or methods do you use in your homeschool?

What do you like about the methods you use?

What do you not like about the methods you use?

Prescription:
Spend some time this week researching various homeschool philosophies on the internet. As you read about them, keep a notepad handy to jot down inspiration from each one. Now use your list to form a homeschool method that's perfect for you and your homeschool. Here are the names of some various homeschool philosophies to get you started:

Classical Education
Charlotte Mason Education
Unschooling
Unit Study Approach
Traditional Homeschool
Waldorf Education
Montessori Education
Interest-Led Homeschooling

Week 28

Therefore, my beloved, as you have always obeyed, so now, not only as in my presence but much more in my absence, work out your own salvation with fear and trembling, for it is God who works in you, both to will and to work for his good pleasure.
—Philippians 2:12-13

The past two weeks we've discussed the role curriculum and homeschooling methods should play in your homeschool. Now it is time to do what Paul advised to the church at Philippi in the above verses.

Much more in the absence of a school telling you what to do.
When you first start homeschooling, I believe the panic is the same for most homeschool moms. What do I do now? I have these wide-eyed children in front of me that I'm expected to educate and I chose to put myself in this situation. Am I crazy? I think this is why most of us run to the safety of curriculum when we are first starting out. Instead of a school telling us what to do, we'll let the curriculum do so. Usually at some point, you run into the same problem that you ran into with schools. The curriculum is asking more of your child than they are capable, or less of your child than they are capable, or to do assignments that seem like nonsensical busy work. Sometimes we cling to homeschool philosophies to help us on our journey and in a way, again, to tell us what we need to do with our children day in and day out because we are fumbling in the dark. We have an idea of how we want to homeschool our children, but there is no magic fairy to come down and make it happen. That's because in the absence of a school, it's up to you.

Work out your own homeschool.
What should our homeschool look like? Julie Bogart, in one of her Brave Writer periscopes, called this process "us-schooling." I love this term because it perfectly describes the end result of the process of finding your homeschool path. You own homeschool will require work to discover what your "us-school" should look like. Explore methods, try curriculum, add a dash of this and some of that, mix ingredients and see what you have. If it doesn't work, keep what you like and try something else. If it works, then continue. Observe your children like they are some rare specimen in the rainforest, which they are; no one else is like them on the entire planet. What do they enjoy? What do they dislike? What drives them? What sparks their imagination and creativity? Can I use that to my advantage in our homeschool? How do I enjoy teaching new information? Hopefully this process is quick since you are around your children all day and have ideas already of what will work and what will not.

God will assist you in your endeavor.
Don't forget, though, that God is with you. He is working in you and your family,

and only wants what is best for all of you. If you continually pray for Him to lead and bless your journey, He will do just that. Always keep in the front of your mind your homeschool mission statement from Week Two in this book and make sure whatever you try aligns with it and with God's will. The end result of manipulating and experimenting with your homeschool is a creation uniquely reflective of our children as learners and you as a teacher.

Diagnosis:
Do you find yourself looking to curriculum, philosophies, or other homeschoolers to tell you what to do in your homeschool? Why?

Do you think it's wise to put so much trust in other influences that know nothing about you and your homeschool, rather than your own knowledge and understanding of your children?

Prescription:
Imagine the perfect homeschool day for your family. Don't focus on attitudes or obedience, but on what you actually would do in your homeschool that day. Write a description of that day below. This is your "un-school".

What stops a day like this from occurring?

Pick a day this week and have nothing on the schedule for the day except the activities and learning experiences you described in the paragraph above. What can you change to make days like this the norm and not the exception?

Week 29

The fear of the Lord is the beginning of knowledge; fools despise wisdom and instruction. —Proverbs 1:7

One of the most chilling passages in all of literature is a scene from The Screwtape Letters where Screwtape is making a toast to start the night of the annual Tempters' Training College banquet. He extols the good job the forces of Satan have done by manipulating education to suit their evil purposes by making public education's attempt to make all equal and not let students achieve their maximum potential, thus making school seem to be a waste of time. Why would this scene open a fictional book about spiritual warfare? Maybe because Satan knows the truth that worthwhile knowledge and wisdom begins with respect for the Lord. It seems the focus on testing in the public schools is leading to a generation who finds no joy and love in learning. As homeschoolers, we need to raise our children to not despise, but love wisdom and knowledge. How do we do this?

Don't expect enjoyment for all subjects.
Sometimes we place burdens on ourselves as homeschool moms that are completely unrealistic, and in my opinion, this is one of them. Your child has his or her own natural talents and interests, thus he or she will not be excited about everything you learn, including entire subjects. This is natural and normal. Do not feel like you are a failure if you child never enjoys math, history, writing, or any other subject you teach. It doesn't mean you shouldn't teach it or try to make it as painless as possible, but don't use your child's reaction when you mention it's time for math as your standard for success.

But do show why all subjects are necessary.
When you have a child who finds certain subjects less than enjoyable, explain to them why they must learn that subject. You could point out the necessity of math in everyday life or the common threads and struggles that run throughout history. You might need to point out that your child's future plans will require a certain number of subjects to be completed for entrance to a university, so if they are interested in pursuing a college education, those two years of foreign language are necessary. Sometimes, as a final straw, I've kindly told my children that part of educating them is the expectation that they will learn how to solve math problems, how to read, and how to write, along with a general knowledge of the world. They don't have to love everything I teach them, but they do need to be respectful and diligent in their work despite their feelings.

Don't dissuade their questions.
The insatiable curiosity of young children is a running joke among parents. The constant "Why?" and "How?" of childhood can be taxing on the most patient of

parents, and the temptation to tune them out or tell your kids to stop is not a good idea. Feed this desire for knowledge by answering their questions to the best of your ability, even if it means writing the question down so you can come back to it at a later time. These questions are the beginning of their education.

But do teach them how to find answers on their own.
As your children get older, probably the most important educational skill you can teach them is how to find answers to their questions. Knowing where and how to find information when needed is a skill that will serve them throughout their life no matter what path they take. From internet searches to books, from online videos to apprenticing with a person, there are innumerable ways in the information age to seek answers and learn about ideas. Make sure your children learn how to exhaust these resources and not to depend upon others to always tell them how to do something. Create self-learners.

Don't stop your own educational endeavors.
My children all know that I attended college and have a bachelor's degree, but that doesn't stop me from continuing to learn. I continue to educate myself in areas where I have an interest in knowing more. Even if you didn't pursue higher education, there are topics that interest us. Continue to learn and explore those subjects that intrigue you.

But do let your children see you continuing to learn.
There is nothing better to inspire your children to love knowledge than letting your children witness your continued education. When they see that learning is a lifelong endeavor to be enjoyed no matter what the age, they too will be inspired. Share what you are learning with your family, whether it's something you learned during Bible study, a new word or phrase in a foreign language you are studying, the final project from your weekly art class, or whatever you are working on. When children are raised in a family culture of the love of knowledge, it will be the natural default throughout their lives.

Diagnosis:
Why do you think knowledge and wisdom must begin with a respect for God?

Does your homeschool foster a love of knowledge and desire for wisdom or a hurried attitude to finish school? How could you change that to a lifestyle of learning?

Have you fallen into the trap of trying to make your child love and enjoy every subject? How is this mindset unrealistic?

Prescription:
Take a week to do nothing but pursue interests with your children. Make a list of ten things you've always wanted to learn or know more about. Have your children make similar lists. Now spend the week learning about and doing items from your lists. Once the week is over, don't let this habit slack. Continue working through each person's list, and create an area where everyone can write questions they have for further research. Answer one question each week. For example, my children asked me how fireworks are made and how they have different colors and designs when they explode. That was our first question we researched together.

1.

2.

3.

4.

5.

6.

7.

8.

9.

10.

Week 30

See to it that no one takes you captive by philosophy and empty deceit, according to human tradition, according to the elemental spirits of the world, and not according to Christ. —Colossians 2:8

One of the things I find troubling about homeschooling in recent years, especially among Christian homeschoolers, is the concern and worry about keeping up with the local school system. I understand why homeschoolers feel this way, but if you are opting to home educate, then there must be something about the public school system that is unacceptable. Don't misunderstand, I have the utmost regard for parents, children, and educators who are involved with the public schools, but even those involved admit our current system is broken, so why would we wish to imitate it or follow their educational standards? The verse above answers this question.

We fall back into the public school mindset and comparisons because it is the human tradition almost all of us know and experienced. It is like comfortable and familiar clothing we can wrap ourselves in when our homeschool seems out of control or our children aren't learning. Just because public school is what we know, doesn't make it any less a human tradition.

In fact, many of the procedures and policies that seem normal to us are actually nothing more than philosophies and empty deceit. For example, why is your grade level determined by the day and year you were born? That seems an arbitrary and odd way to determine who should be grouped together to learn. And why, based upon your grade, are all students in that age range expected to know and achieve certain educational milestones? We all know students learn at different rates and don't fit into perfect standardized boxes. Don't force your own homeschooled children into these boxes because of a misguided attempt to keep up with the school system.

Even if our modern educational structure didn't have flaws, its intention is to instruct children in worldly wisdom and not according to Christ. Whether or not you agree that religious instruction has no place in public schools, it has always been commanded by God to occur in the home. Our modern school system is not designed to teach or practice the Christian faith, and looking to the school system as a guide for what to teach in our Christian homeschools seems a little bit strange.

Disclaimer: I have nothing against the public school system. I do believe it has serious problems that need to be addressed, however, I used to be a teacher, and I come from a family of teachers and administrators. I also know there are plenty of good, Christian teachers who try to make a difference in their students' lives within the legal constraints placed upon them. This devotional is meant to help us think about why we continue to turn to the public school system for guidance when we have chosen to not use that institution to educate our children.

Diagnosis:
Do you have a tendency to look at the schools to judge if your children are on track with their learning? Why or why not?

What problems do you see in the public schools that you can correct by homeschooling your children?

Prescription:
This week weed out any areas in your homeschool that are too influenced by a public school mindset. Usually these areas also cause stress and frustration in your homeschool too, however, if some schoolish holdovers are working for you, then, of course, keep them (my kids love eating off lunch trays and having a lunch menu posted every week). Some questions to ask:

1. Are you teaching some subjects because you feel you should to keep up?

2. Is your daily schedule and/or homeschool area based on a public school classroom?

3. Do you feel every page and every question in every book must be completed even if your child already understands?

4. Do you assign book reports, journal writing, and reports because public schools do?

5. Are you constantly checking the school standards to see if your grade level child has learned everything they "should"?

Week 31

To put off your old self...and to be renewed in the spirit of your minds, and to put on the new self... —Ephesians 4:22a-24a

If you've been homeschooling for any amount of time, from a few months to many years, then you've found yourself in a situation where the curriculum or approach you've chosen is not working for you, your children, or your family. There's nothing worse than feeling you've wasted money and having to start over mid-year. Sometimes, though, having things go wrong during your school year can actually be a process to move your homeschool in the right direction. These verses give us a basic outline for when change is necessary.

Put off your old self.
Usually this step is the most difficult in the entire process. Admitting things aren't working can send homeschool moms in a panic. Should I even be homeschooling because I'm struggling and my children are struggling? How can I buy more curriculum when I'm low on funds and it might not work either? Why is our homeschool not the peaceful learning oasis I envisioned? Seeking the answers to questions that arise when you realize there are problems is how you put off the old. It doesn't mean you are a failure or a horrible judge of what curriculum your child needs. Read this carefully: there is not one homeschooler out there who hasn't had to change things in their homeschool at least once, and most likely multiple times.

Renewed in the spirit of your mind.
Once you've accepted the need for a change, it's time to renew your mind. The quickest way is to spend time in prayer, specifically asking God to lead you to other homeschoolers who can help provide suggestions and curriculum advice. The other renewal on which to focus is something you probably already know. There is no perfect curriculum that will correct all the problems in your homeschool. Don't fall into the cycle of searching for the perfect when it doesn't exist. In fact, sometimes it's not even a problem that needs to be fixed by changing curriculum at all.

Put on the new self.
At this point in the process, you've accepted the need to change and made the necessary changes. Now turn your attention to putting on your new self. Just like in life, making changes in your homeschool takes time and grace. Usually I get super excited when it's time to start new curriculum, a new schedule, or other changes in our homeschool. Unfortunately, I tend to forget that there is always an adjustment period for me and for the kids. The worst thing you can do is decide during this adjustment period to scrap what you've already changed and start over. I try to give myself at least three to four months before I assess whether the

changes corrected the problem. If not, I start the process again.

Realizing something in your homeschool needs to change is not a failure on your part, but adjusting to the needs of your family.

Diagnosis:
What holds you back from making changes in your homeschool? Or do you have the opposite problem of changing things too often?

Is discovering a curriculum doesn't work truly a waste of money? Why or why not? (Consider this quote by Edison when asked about inventing the light bulb: "I have not failed. I have just found 10,000 ways that won't work.").

Have you found you expect changes to bring instant positive results? Is this realistic?

Why is renewing your mind such an important part of the process of change in your homeschool?

Prescription:
Observe your homeschool this week to see if there are any changes in curriculum, schedules, habits, storage, or whatever that need to be made. Jot down any areas of contention that you see reoccurring. It could be a child that cries every time a certain book comes off the shelf, constant arguing over pencils, crayons, etc., or possibly a subject you never get to because of where it's placed in your daily schedule. Follow the steps outlined above to try to solve any consistent problems you notice.

Week 32

Therefore, since we are surrounded by so great a cloud of witnesses, let us also lay aside every weight, and sin which clings so closely, and let us run with endurance the race that is set before us. —Hebrews 12:1

As homeschooling grows more and more every year, the number of homeschool moms grows as well. The benefits of this "cloud of witnesses" are many, but let's look at just a few this week.

Who is our cloud of witnesses?
Every homeschool mom needs to find her own personal cloud of witnesses, other homeschool moms who have children the same age or older than your own children. Sometimes it can feel lonely when you go against the grain, and it doesn't hurt to have other people in your corner with you.

Where do you find a cloud of witnesses?
The easiest place to find fellow homeschoolers is at local homeschool co-ops or groups. The combination of proximity and having a united goal makes this a really fabulous option because there is nothing quite like some face-to-face homeschool chats. However, it is even possible to find homeschoolers through the internet as well. On social media websites and internet forums, you can find homeschoolers who fit with your particular religious group, your specific curriculum choice, homeschool methodology, and any other designation you desire. Another option is to attend a homeschool convention at some point during the year, and immerse yourself in nothing but sheer homeschool bliss for two or three days. Of course if all else fails, head to your local library during school hours and watch for a mom with school age children. Most likely, they are homeschoolers.

Why do you need a cloud of witnesses?
The verse above tells us why we need our own homeschool cloud of witnesses, to help us lay aside the burdens of homeschooling and run with endurance this race that is set before us. I have found an unbelievable amount of help, guidance, encouragement, and inspiration from various homeschool moms I've met in real life and online. It is so helpful to have someone to ask for solutions when problems arise or suggestions about curriculum choices. It is encouraging to have homeschool moms who inspire you to continue through to the end because they've already walked this path. We all need the support and guidance that comes from other homeschool moms who are in the trenches with us every day educating our children.

Diagnosis:
Do you have a cloud of witnesses in your life that you can turn to for support or advice? Why do you think it's beneficial?

What specific situations have you called upon your fellow homeschool moms for help?

Prescription:
While it's important for you to have support, it's also important for homeschool kids to feel that they are part of a group as well. If you haven't already, make it a point to seek out some fellow homeschoolers with whom your children can interact on a regular basis. I noticed that as my oldest hit those tween/teen years she suddenly needed much more social interaction than she had previously. There's no harm in starting this search early if you and your family wish. I know my children have greatly enjoyed meeting other homeschool children. It helps them to not feel so alone, too.

They are not of the world, just as I am not of the world. Sanctify them in the truth; your word is truth. As you sent me into the world, so I have sent them into the world.

—John 17:16-18

ast year I saw the above verses being used as motivation by a parent as the reason to not homeschool their son. The reasoning was something along the lines that since Christians are to live in the world, then homeschooling would be taking them out of the world. It struck me as a strange rationale, but not one I haven't heard before. Many Christian parents feel that their children need to be in the public school system to act as shining lights in an otherwise, all too often, dark, sinful place. While parents definitely should do what they feel is best, the above verses are actually a pattern of discipleship for Christians who are young in their faith.

Your children are not meant to be in this world.
For that matter none of us are. We are designed to be with God, which is what Christianity is all about— being able to return to God at the end of our lives. The Bible talks of us as sojourners and exiles on this earth (1 Peter 2:11-12). Our conduct and beliefs are supposed to be so different from those around us that we stand out as unique by our behavior and attitudes. The problem is that when children are thrown into an environment with other children their age for eight hours a day, 180 days a year, then the odds are much more in favor of your children behaving and acting more like the ones they are around for the bulk of the day. I'm not saying it's impossible, but it will take much more work during the four or so hours you have with them after school to impress upon them your values and faith.

Until they have been sanctified in Truth.
Before Jesus sent his apostles out to change the world with their message, they spent three years listening to Jesus teach the Truth. They had time to learn and mature. Jesus even supervised their apprenticeship by sending them out with explicit instructions of how to conduct themselves and what to do (Mark 6:7-13). Don't forget that these were grown men, but they still needed three years to learn all they would need to interact with the world and the spiritual battles they would face. Many times parents send their children to school with the mission of being lights to their peers at the age of five. How much sanctification in the Truth could they have had at that point?

Then they are to be sent into the world.
Ultimately, Christians are meant to spread the Gospel message to the world. We are expected to interact with others in our neighborhoods and towns. We

are commanded to share our faith everywhere we go (Matthew 28:19-20). Our children need to know how to navigate in the world as well, but homeschooling solves the problems that present themselves with the first two items in the equation. Homeschool parents can slow the exposure of their children to worldly influences until it is more age appropriate, and they can make sure they have been saturated in the Truth until they are sent into the world. Our children will be sent into the world one way or another. Wouldn't you rather make sure they are spiritually ready when you send them?

Diagnosis:
What is your opinion about sending out children to be lights among their peers in a public school setting?

Does it make a difference if we protect our children from the world as much as possible until they have learned truth? What would be the difference?

Prescription:
Think of ways you can actively prepare your children to face the world. Some ideas would be apologetics, service projects, personal Bible study, etc. Choose one of your ideas to implement this week.

Week 34

Now, therefore, thus says the Lord of hosts: Consider your ways. You have sown much, and harvested little. You eat, but you never have enough; you drink, but you never have your fill. You clothe yourselves, but no one is warm...Thus says the Lord of hosts: Consider your ways. —Haggai 1:5-7

At the end of each class in college, the professor hands out an evaluation form where students are asked to critique the professor and the class. I'm assuming these evaluations are used to help the professor improve the class and his teaching style, or possibly, they are just tossed in the trash! While our homeschools are definitely not a formal educational setting, it is always helpful to "consider your ways" as the verses above say, and let your children do their own evaluation form of your homeschool year. Why?

To be an effective educator. In the verses above, the prophet Haggai talks about sowing much, and harvesting little; drinking, but never being full; being clothed, but not being warm. Basically, he's talking about wasting your time. Sometimes as homeschool moms, we find ourselves at the end of the year feeling that we've done a lot, but little has been accomplished. One possibility is that we're being too hard on ourselves and in actuality quite a bit has been accomplished, but we can't see it. This is why it's important to make goals (Week 2) and to record our homeschool successes no matter how small (Week 4). Another possibility is that the curriculum you are using is not a good fit for your child. They may have trouble retaining information because the information is being presented in a way that does not "click" for that child, leading to much time being spent with little success. Letting your children in on the process of evaluating the homeschool year will also give you better insight into how they learn and what makes learning enjoyable for them.

To help your children have ownership over their education. My favorite part of homeschooling is definitely the planning. I love to sit down with a blank piece of paper and begin to figure out exactly what we'll study in the coming year. However, I'm not educating myself, and it's proven much more effective during our school year to let the children assist in some of the planning for the coming year. It is their education after all and their "ways" are the ones for which I'm trying to prepare them.

To brainstorm ideas. I don't know why, but I continued to be shocked at some of the great ideas my kids have shared over how to organize and schedule our homeschool. Once you've spotted some areas where you could be more efficient or more organized with your day, let your children take part in helping find a solution. First, they will probably be more creative and think outside the box than you do.

Secondly, if you let them have some say in how the routines work in your homeschool, the odds are better that they won't fuss about sticking to them.

Diagnosis:
Have you ever let your children evaluate your homeschool year?

Why do you think taking time to really talk to your children about their homeschool education would be helpful?

Prescription:
This week take some time to talk to your children about how they believe the educational year went. I am providing you a list of questions on the next page to give you some ideas of what to ask. You can do this however you wish, but I do have some recommendations.

First, talk to each child individually. If you try to do it with all your children at once, I find that usually the kids just agree with whoever answered first, and you don't really discern their individual opinions. Secondly, with younger children (K-2), focus mainly on the first three questions. The other questions will probably be too difficult for them to answer. Finally, let your children know that whatever they say, even if it's a criticism, will not get them in trouble, but you'll listen with an open mind. They need to know you are truly wanting their opinion as long as it's presented in a respectful way.

As an example, here's how we do our yearly evaluation. I schedule a time with one of my kids, take them to our local coffee shop, just the two of us, and we talk through the questions on the next page. I make notes as they share. It's really that simple, but it's a huge help when it comes time to flesh out what we're doing the next year and create goals.

Yearly Homeschool Evaluation

1) What was your favorite subject we studied? Why?

2) What was your least favorite subject? Why?

3) What would you like to learn about?

4) What would you like to do differently in our daily routine or the subjects we study?

5) What do you feel you struggle with the most?

6) What do you feel are your strengths?

7) Name one goal you would like to achieve next year (educationally, physically and/or spiritually)?

8) Rank the following in order of perference of how you like to learn, with 1 being your favorite. Each section will have a number one.

Section One:

___Individual

___With Siblings

___One-on-One with Mom

Section Two:

___Worksheets/workbooks

___Reading

___Watching documentaries or educational videos

___Hands-on (projects/experiments)

___Notebooking or lapbooking

Week 35

Not that I have already obtained this or am already perfect, but I press on to make it my own, because Christ Jesus has made me his own. Brothers, I do not consider that I have made it my own. But one thing I do: forgetting what lies behind and straining forward to what lies ahead, I press on toward the goal for the prize of the upward call of God in Christ Jesus. —Philippians 3:12-14

It's coming to the close of another homeschool year and after going through all of these devotionals and challenges, you might be feeling like you had a good year, but still have a lot of work to do in some areas of your homeschool and yourself. Guess what? Everyone does. No one is perfect this side of heaven, which is exactly what the verses above discuss.

Not that I have already obtained this or am already perfect

You are a constant work in progress. Your children are a work in progress, as is your homeschool. What works for all of you this year, might not work next year. There were some years, especially when my children were small, that our homeschool changed the way it looked every month! One promise I can make you is that your homeschool will never be perfect. We keep striving and working to improve ourselves and the way our homeschool works, but don't be upset that perfection is not happening.

I press on to make it my own

Your homeschool should reflect you and your family, not some arbitrary standard or another family. Keep pressing on until you find your sweet spot of home education. Make your homeschool your own and be confident in the individuality and customization that represents. Don't let anyone make you feel less than for doing what works.

Forgetting what lies behind

Probably the most difficult part for me at the close of a school year is dwelling on all of the things I wish I'd done better: my attitude, finishing our curriculum, focusing on habit training with the kids, etc. However, the past is in the past, and unless I want to wallow in misery and regret during our school break, it's best to follow the advice above, forget what lies behind. A new school year will be upon you soon enough where you can make changes and adjust what you feel was lacking. Carrying around a burden from the previous years of all that went wrong is neither healthy nor productive.

Straining forward to what lies ahead

At the beginning of the year, you made some goals for your homeschool in general and for your children specifically. Don't lose sight of those goals as the year ends. Those are the goals you are working to achieve. You surely had struggles this year, but I promise you are closer to what you want for your homeschool and for your children than you were at the beginning of the year. Keep looking ahead and focus there.

The goal for the prize of the upward call of God in Christ Jesus
While it's beneficial to assess how well you achieved the academic goals each year, the best goal to analyze is THE goal: Heaven. Are your children closer to God at the end of the school year? Are you closer to God? Have certain attitudes or character issues been improved upon in both yourself and the children? Did you include service projects in your year so your children show the love of Christ to others? Too often we lose sight of the prize because we're focused on the other runners or the spectators. Don't lose the eternal prize for an earthly education.

Diagnosis:
Does the end of the homeschool year make you a little hard on yourself about what you accomplished or didn't accomplish? Why?

What is the hardest part of these verses for you personally? Do you feel like a failure if you or your homeschool isn't perfect? Are you making your homeschool personalized instead of comparing to others? Do you forgive yourself for mistakes you made during the year? Have you kept your goals in sight? Is heaven still your main goal?

Prescription:
Look back at the goals you created at the beginning of this book for each of your children. Re-read your homeschool mission statement. How did your year compare to the goals and mission statement you made?

Where do you feel you could do better with your goals? How could you correct those problems for the next school year?

Was your homeschool effective at focusing on THE goal this year? How or how not?

Week 36

God is not man, that he should lie, or a son of man, that he should change his mind. Has he said, and will he not do it? Or has he spoken, and will he not fulfill it?

—Numbers 23:19

Many years ago when I was in college, I had some life experiences that shook me to my core and threatened to destroy my floundering faith once and for all. I chose to approach God as a last ditch effort to fix my life and find healing. I would spend an hour every day between classes in one of the study rooms at the library reading and studying my Bible, meditating, and praying. One night, I was lying in bed and I felt totally broken and stripped bare. I could feel the overwhelming pressure of what God expected from me. The more time I spent in the Word, the more I could see how sinful I truly was. I cried out to God in prayer with tears streaming down my face that I didn't think I could do what He asked. I wasn't strong enough to follow Him. I was too broken and sinful to be transformed into His image. There were just too many things I needed to fix about myself. When I awoke the next morning, the first thought that entered my head was the following: "I don't need you to fix things or transform yourself. I will do that, but I need you to trust me and humble yourself to my care."

I've never forgotten that moment or how close God felt to me at that point.

I find myself often recalling that time in my life as I homeschool my children. I've decided that for many of us, the struggles we have with homeschooling are the result of trying to fix what is broken in our homeschools instead of giving it to God. Do we really trust Him to take care of our children? Do we really have faith that He will make all things work together for good? We say it, but do we really mean it; do we live it? If we do truly have faith in Him and His promises, then our worry, anxiety, and stress level should be zero or close to it. Let's look at three of God's promises a little more closely as we close out this year:

Read 1 Peter 5:6-7

There are two commands for us in these verses and two promises of God. First, we are to humble ourselves. As homeschoolers, this is where we completely yield to His leading and guidance in our homeschool. God knows best, and I am His vessel. When we truly humble ourselves, He will exalt us at the proper time. Maybe others see the evidence in your children of how accomplished and spiritual they are, so they heap blessings upon your head, or maybe you are not exalted until the next life, but God promises that when we submit, He will lift. The second command is for us to cast all of our anxieties on Him. Homeschool moms have plenty of anxiety. God wants it. He wants you to give Him all of your anxiety about your children, your marriage, your homeschool, your life because He cares about you. He doesn't want you to carry around a load of anxiety. If you give Him those anxieties, He promises to let that burden be His and not yours any longer.

Read Philippians 1:6
God started your family down this path of homeschooling, and in this verse He has promised to bring that good work to completion. The end of your homeschool journey may be different than mine, but God has promised to be with us until the end. You will never homeschool alone, even if you homeschool for only a year or for thirteen years. God is with you, day in and day out, helping you complete this good work.

Read Matthew 7:11
The prime motivation for all the homeschool moms I know is a love for our children. We are homeschooling because we know that it is best for them. This verse tell us that if we, as fallen, sinful human beings, know how to do good things for our children out of love for them, how much more will God do for them out of His holy, perfect love. I must admit that this verse gives me the most comfort of all. I cannot imagine loving my children more than I do, but God does. I cannot imagine wanting more for them out of this life, and God has plans for them. I cannot imagine desiring more than I already do that they will one day all choose to be followers of Christ as well, but God has desired that before the foundations of the earth. No matter how much I do for them, God does more and will do more.

Diagnosis:
Do you homeschool like you believe the promises God makes in these three passages of scripture?

Which of these promises do you struggle with the most (God loves and cares for your children more than you, God will make sure your homeschool is completed, God will exalt you if you humble yourself, or God will take care of all your anxieties)? Why?

Prescription:
Pour out your heart to God through a letter or prayer about having faith in His promises about your homeschool. Be honest about how you've struggled with this and ask for His help with depending on His might and love

For the Weeks You
Are Not Homeschooling

Week 1

And Peter answered Him, "Lord if it is you, command me to come to you on the water."
He said, "Come." So Peter got out of the boat and walked on the water and came to
Jesus. But when he saw the wind, he was afraid, and beginning to sink he cried out,
"Lord, save me." Jesus immediately reached out his hand and took hold of him, saying
to him, "O you of little faith, why did you doubt?" —Matthew 14:28-31

My children loved watching Veggietales when they were younger, and the opening line of each cartoon said, "Why we do what we do." Every homeschooler has a "why we do what we do" moment. It was that moment when you stepped out of the comfort of the public or private school boat and into the stormy path of doing things differently for your family by homeschooling. I'm not sure what your moment was, but mine came before my kids were even school age. The final "get out of the boat" moment was when I subbed in our local school system while pregnant with our second child. I knew by the end of the day my kids were not going to attend there. I had officially stepped out of the boat.

Once you've made the decision to walk on the stormy seas, it isn't smooth sailing. Now you have those distractions raging all around you that call to you and make you doubt that first step over the side. What about testing? What about socialization? What about antagonistic family and friends? What about high school? What about my child being behind or ahead? The swirling sound of questioning and doubting voices around you and in your own head is too much to bear. And all you can do is cry, "Lord, save me!"

Then you imagine Him standing in front of you with His hand outstretched. He shakes His head and asks us why we doubt. Did He not call us out of the boat, and if He called us, will He not equip us with all that we need (Hebrews 13:21)?

When I find myself in the position of treading water in our homeschool as doubts and fear creep into my daily life, I know one thing; I'm ignoring His hand. I've lost my focus. My eyes have left the one who equips, and I'm focused on the voices that destroy. I've forgotten why I stepped out of the boat. I'm believing the lies that rage around me about my decision to homeschool. It is time for me reach up and cling tightly to His hand, and to remember that the entire reason I'm walking this stormy path is to bring my children closer to Him.

Diagnosis:
What was your "get out of the boat" moment?

What do you fear the most?

I find homeschool doubts creep into my life in direct correlation to how much I'm letting my quiet time with the Lord wane. Do you find this to be true for you?

Prescription:
This week write down the distractions you feel surrounding you that try to drag you under the water during your homeschool days. The distraction of clutter? The wave of worry? The crash of criticism? Write out a prayer describing what makes you sink and how you feel. Now read the following verses about having faith in God: 1 John 5:5; Mark 11:24; Matthew 21:21; and Hebrews 11:1. Finish your prayer by recording how these verses help you deal with your homeschool distractions.

Week 2

Abide in me and I in you. As the branch cannot bear fruit by itself, unless it abides in the vine, neither can you, unless you abide in me. I am the vine; you are the branches. Whoever abides in me and I in him, he it is that bears much fruit, for apart from me you can do nothing. —John 15:4-5

I am sure we've all seen what happens to leaves or flowers once they've been plucked from the plant or tree; they begin to die. We can place them in a vase of water, which might slow the inevitable, but death is a matter of time. Jesus uses this picture in the verses above to stress the importance of staying connected to Him. All too often I find myself letting that connection sever due to the busyness and craziness of motherhood and homeschooling. However, this is the worst possible scenario for homeschool moms who are already responsible for educating their children.

We must abide to be fruitful.

Want your homeschooling day to go well? Abide in Him. Need more peace, kindness, and self-control in your home? Abide in Him. If our desire is to be fruitful with our children's education, fruitful in our family relationships, and fruitful with our spiritual lives, then the only option is to abide in Jesus. No other option exists for Christians. According to Jesus' words, there is a direct correlation between our abiding and our fruitfulness. In fact, Jesus promises us that if we don't abide, our ability to achieve will be zero.

We must abide in Jesus.

Probably my biggest struggle with abiding is not my setting aside the time to do so, but spending that time abiding in the wrong things. Jesus is very clear that when we abide, it must be in Him. Unfortunately, all too often I pause with Jesus and abide elsewhere. The word abide in these verses is menó in Greek, which carries with it the meaning of remaining and staying. I abide with blogs that help me learn more about homeschooling resources and ideas. I abide with books and magazines to help me be a better mom. All the while, Jesus may as well be standing in the corner jumping and waving his hands trying to get my attention, "Hey, Chelli! If you'll just abide in me, I'll take care of all your concerns and make your endeavors fruitful. Spend some real time with Me meditating on scripture, studying the word, and pouring your heart out to me. Abide in ME!"

The answer to all of our worries and struggles is such a simple one, like many things in the Bible. It's simply to abide, to live, and to dwell in connection with Jesus. I want to show that example to my children, a mother who abides in her Lord.

Diagnosis:
Do you set aside time each day to abide with Jesus on a personal level? How much?

Do you find yourself searching for answers and encouragement from places other than Jesus and His Word more often than you are spending in quiet time with Him?

Why do you think Jesus makes abiding in him such a black and white area? Why is it so important?

Prescription:
Start the habit this week of setting aside a larger amount of time to abide with Jesus through meditation, Bible reading, prayer, singing songs of praise, and Bible study. It doesn't all need to be at the same time (some days it's difficult to find ten minutes you can have alone!), but it does need to add up over the course of the day. Record the positive benefits you see in your day from consciously practicing abiding in Jesus. Keep it up during your school weeks as well!

Week 3

Count it all joy, my brothers, when you meet trials of various kinds, for you know that the testing of your faith produces steadfastness, And let steadfastness have its full effect, that you may be perfect and complete lacking in nothing. —James 1:2-4

I truly believe homeschooling has made me a better Christian. Not because it's provided tons of time for fasting and meditation, but because it's provided plenty of time and opportunity for the Lord to bring the least Christ-like parts of myself to the surface.

As you spend your days attempting to teach your children, you are guaranteed to meet various trials and have your faith tested: the trials of struggling students, poor attitudes, and living on a limited budget; the testing of your faith because you're uncertain if it will all work out; and your doubts about God's ability to truly provide for your children's future in spite of your shortcomings.

These tests and trials produce a steadfastness, because once God has broken down your walls, you realize your inadequacy to be all that your children need as a teacher. At that point, you are left only with Him to steadfastly cling.

Now God has you in a place where he can work on your soul, your character, and your heart. He can bring you forward into a mature Christian walk where you lack in nothing because He has filled those doubts and worries with the surety of His care.

How is homeschooling uniquely suited to bring about these changes? I believe it's because as homeschool moms, there are no other feet at which we can lay our child's successes or failures but our own. When you feel the pressure, not only of motherhood, but also of sole educator, it's only a matter of time before the ugliness inside you bubbles to the surface, just like the pressure in the earth causes magma to bubble to the surface in a volcanic eruption.

The end result of this pressurized atmosphere is one of two things: you don't give control to God and try to run your homeschool on your own strength, or you steadfastly cling to Him and He gives back completeness to your homeschool that you could never find otherwise.

Diagnosis:
Do you find that homeschooling has shined a light into some areas of your life that are still not Christ-like? Which ones?

Why do you think homeschooling helps us grow in Christ?

How does viewing the struggles you have in homeschooling as a way to perfect your faith help you see those struggles differently?

Prescription:
Share these verses with your children about how trials and tests are used by God to draw us closer to him due to our dependence on Him in these times. Ask them for examples or give examples of times when they've struggled that God could be trying to teach them how to be more like Christ and closer to Him. This week make it a family challenge that when struggles and trials arise that everyone tries to look at the deeper spiritual meaning of what they need to learn about themselves.

Week 4

Now as they were on their way, Jesus entered a village. And a woman named Martha welcomed him into her house. And she had a sister called Mary, who sat at the Lord's feet and listened to his teaching. But Martha was distracted with much serving. And she went up to him and said, "Lord, do you not care that my sister has left me to serve alone? Tell her then to help me." But the Lord answered her, "Martha, Martha, you are anxious and troubled about many things, but one thing is necessary. Mary has chosen the good portion, which will not be taken away from her." —Luke 10:38-42

The story of Mary and Martha is one that is familiar to most women. It is generally used to contrast the focus of the two: Mary focused on Christ, and Martha focused on earthly concerns. While this story has nothing to do with homeschooling, it is one of my favorite Bible passages that inspires, teaches, and encourages me as a homeschool mom.

All too often, I find myself on the Martha side of the equation. In fact, my overwhelming Martha tendencies led me down the path to learn how to be more of a Mary in our homeschool. So what would Mary and Martha be like if they were homeschool mothers?

Mary	Martha
• Focuses on the hearts and character of herself and her children.	• Focuses on academic standards and how well her children compare to other children academically.
• Uses academics to point to God and serve Him.	• Uses academics to point to future career plans and money-making potential.
• Shows the patience and love of God through her attitude and how she deals with academic struggles.	• Shows the wrath and judgment of God through her attitude and how she deals with academic struggles.
• Prays over her homeschool every day.	• Too busy to consistently pray or spend time in Bible study.
• Prioritizes good habits in spiritual, physical, and emotional matters.	• Prioritizes keeping up with the schedule, other homeschoolers, public schools, or private schools.
• Makes her homeschool one of restful learning.	• Makes her homeschool one of deadlines, worry, and stress.

After reading these lists, I still find myself with quite a few affirmatives on the Martha side. But the wonderful part of Mary and Martha's story is that Jesus doesn't condemn Martha for her request for assistance in the kitchen. Jesus merely tells her what Mary is doing is better, more important, than Martha's concerns.

I believe the same is true of Homeschool Mary and Homeschool Martha. Martha's focus and concerns are not necessarily bad, but they aren't as beneficial and eternity-focused as Mary's. That thought helps this Martha breathe a sigh of relief. I can still have my Martha tendencies; I just need to choose to sit at Jesus' feet more and alter my focus more. I need to focus on being a Mary more every day because there is something better out there for my homeschool and my children if I choose to be Mary.

Diagnosis:
Who do you find yourself resembling more in your homeschool, Mary or Martha? Why do you think this is the case?

What are some things Jesus might tell you that you are troubled about in your homeschool? What would be the one thing He would tell you is necessary?

Prescription:
Look at each of the items on the Mary and Martha lists. Obviously we want to be as much like Mary as possible, so be honest with yourself about the triggers that send you into Martha territory. Is it something you hear about a neighbor child's academic achievements? The fear your child will never learn how to read? For each item on Martha's side, list one scenario that makes you morph into Martha. Now list a way that you could counteract your thinking and remain on the Mary side of things. Practice these tricks all week while interacting with your children.

Week 5

I therefore, a prisoner for the Lord, urge you to walk in a manner worthy of the calling to which you have been called, with all humility and gentleness, with patience, bearing with one another in love, eager to maintain the unity of the Spirit in the bond of peace. —Ephesians 4:1-3

I love this passage of scripture! I call it the homeschool mom's job description. Everything outlined in these verses is what our goal should be for ourselves in our homeschool, so we'll be looking at this passage next week as well. This week, let's focus on verse one.

Urge you to walk in a manner worthy of your calling

William Shakespeare wrote in his play Twelfth Night, "Some are born great, some achieve greatness, and some have greatness thrust upon them." Many times homeschoolers fit in these same three categories: some have known since their children were born that they wanted to homeschool; some slowly warm to the idea; and some are suddenly thrust into it due to circumstances beyond their control. However you became a homeschool mom, you are to walk that path in a worthy manner. So what exactly does it look like to homeschool in a worthy manner?

If I'm homeschooling in a worthy manner...

I treat it seriously. As much as I hate to admit it, homeschooling is our job. The state trusts us to raise educated citizens. While the flexibility of homeschooling is one of the biggest perks, repeatedly canceling school because you are tired or don't feel like it today is not acceptable. When you treat educating your children cavalierly, you damage their future, because at some point, you run out of time. Since I struggle with this, one thing I ask myself is, "If my child had a teacher in public school who taught as consistently as I do, would I be pleased?" Caveat: This doesn't mean you need to swing too far the other way of being draconian in your approach. Balance, always balance.

I do whatever is best for my child and my family. I love homeschooling and truly believe the home education model solves most of the problems in the public school system today. However, as a homeschool mom, you need to always keep in the forefront of your mind that your homeschool approach and even your decision to homeschool, might vary from child to child or year to year. Sometimes we cling so tightly to homeschooling that we won't even consider public school, private school, or outsourcing some classes, even if it might be best for our children.

I fully rely on God. Despite how many books and blogs we read about being effective homeschool moms, no matter how well I educate my children, even if

I've laid the best religious foundation I can, ultimately, I must depend on God. I will never love my children more or want more for them in this life than He does. I am an imperfect creation and even my best efforts will fall short, but God is there to make up the difference, to fill in the spaces I have missed, to supply what my children need as they need it.

Home education is a big responsibility, and we need walk in a way that would glorify Him.

Diagnosis:
Do you take homeschooling seriously enough or too seriously? Why?

If doing what was best for your family required you to quit homeschooling or drastically change the way you homeschool, would you feel like a failure? Why?

How does relying on God play out in your homeschool?

Prescription:
Write a paragraph telling what walking worthily as a homeschool mom means to you. Hang on to this paragraph since you will be adding to it next week.

Week 6

I therefore, a prisoner for the Lord, urge you to walk in a manner worthy of the calling to which you have been called, with all humility and gentleness, with patience, bearing with one another in love, eager to maintain the unity of the Spirit in the bond of peace. —Ephesians 4:1-3

Let's jump right in and examine the rest of the homeschool mom mantra.

With all humility, gentleness, patience, bearing with one another in love
How different, but how necessary this list is for homeschool moms. We need to realize that our child's academic successes are not our work, but God's work through our flaws. We need to have gentleness in the tone of our voices and the touch of our hands when navigating our children over academic struggles. We need more patience while teaching that lesson one more time even though we thought it had been mastered weeks ago. We need to realize we bear with all of this crazy homeschool lifestyle because of love for the people under our roof. Because of all this we are...

Eager to maintain the unity of the Spirit in the bond of peace
The word eager here in the original Greek means to move quickly by fully applying oneself. We must move quickly and with all our strength and determination so that we may maintain unity in our home, unity between family members, and unity with God. We know that this unity is more important than crying about math or frustration over reading or helplessness about writing. Our peace and our home's peace flow from how much unity is present, so we never allow strife, discord, nor apathy to eat away at those bonds. We rush eagerly with the Spirit's help to repair our peace.

If only I could describe myself this way! While I cannot say this is what I'm like as a homeschool mom, it should be what I strive to attain. My children would be most blessed to have a mom who homeschools them in this manner.

Diagnosis:
Where do you struggle most in your homeschool day? With humility, gentleness, or patience?

Why do you think there is a direct correlation between unity and peace?

Prescription:
Last week you wrote a paragraph about walking worthily as a homeschool mom. This week add a second paragraph to the first about the importance of humility, gentleness, patience, and unity in your homeschool day. Consider these paragraphs your inspiration and your challenge for the homeschool year and years to come.

Week 7

It is better to live in a corner of the housetop than in a house shared with a quarrelsome wife. —Proverbs 21:9

We've all heard the phrase, "If momma ain't happy, ain't nobody happy." Basically the verse above is expressing the same sentiment with much more poetic language. Throughout this book I've mentioned that homeschool moms need to be considerate of how we act and react when teaching our children so we don't ruin our relationship with them.

Sometimes, however, we just wake up in a bad mood or not feeling the best. It's not due to stress, worries, or struggles with our children's education, but a generally grouchy demeanor. Unfortunately, I find that when my mood goes south, it's usually because I've let some of the basics of self-care slide for too long.

Do a quick check of these areas when you find yourself so quarrelsome that everyone wants to move to the corner of the roof.

1. Am I getting enough sleep? I know that as moms we all have seasons in life, especially when we have babies in the home, where this answer is no, and there is not much you can do about it. However, some of us (me!) are also night owls and want to enjoy the silence and solitude of a house in slumber to have some alone time. Be careful, though, because staying up too late can cause a quarrelsome mother the next day.

2. Am I eating healthy, filling food? I'm not saying you need to stick to a strict diet, but it is true that certain foods make us feel more energized and motivated, while others make us feel like a bloated cow. You might have been indulging in too much comfort food and not in enough fruits, vegetables, and protein, so you are feeling out of sorts.

3. Am I engaging in some kind of exercise? Again, I don't expect you to get up at the crack of dawn and jog five miles. I'm definitely not doing that! But exercise does make us feel better and releases endorphins in our brain, which puts us in a better frame of mind. One quick way I snagged some exercise this past spring was to wear my exercise clothes and sneakers while teaching the kids. While they were working on something, or even while I was teaching, I'd stand up and march in place or do squats, jumping jacks, arm weights, etc. Two birds with one stone!

4. Am I connected to my husband and friends? As an extrovert, one of the biggest mood destroyers for me is to be without adult conversation for too long. I need to stay connected to my husband, not only for our marriage, but also for my sanity. I also need to be with friends on a regular basis so I can relax and enjoy some downtime to just be me.

5. Am I connected to my children? This might sound strange considering I'm a homeschool mom, but it's easy to lose your connection to your children despite being with them all day long. I have to make a conscious effort to seek them out at the end of the school day to spend some time with them as mom instead of teacher. If I go too long without making that effort, my children begin to act up and I begin to react instead of being proactive.

6. Am I abiding in God? In an earlier chapter of this section I emphasized the necessity of abiding with God. If I'm particularly quarrelsome, I can pretty much promise that it's because my spiritual life is struggling. Make sure to make time to abide.

7. Am I prepared to teach? I don't know if this is a side effect of my planning, type A personality, but if I start our school day and find myself constantly having to search for items we need or print something off the computer that should have been printed the night before, my quarrelsome meter can go from zero to sixty in about a millisecond. I have to prepare for the next day the night before or that morning before we start school or everyone will be on the corner of the house to get away from me for sure!

8. Is it just one of those days? Sometimes there is nothing on this list that has me in a funk; it's just one of those days. When that happens, I call off school for the day. We might lay around and read, watch some documentaries, or take a neighborhood walk, but no formal school work. I consider these mental health days. While it's unwise to take too many of these, having an occasional day off now and then to keep everyone sane is a great idea.

Once you've gone through this list and pinpointed what has you so grouchy, by all means, take every step you can to remedy the situation and keep everybody under the roof instead of on it!

Diagnosis:
Does you being quarrelsome or waking up on the wrong side of the bed affect your school day?

What items could you add to the list that make you quarrelsome?

Prescription:
Since we all know that off days will happen, take some time during this break week to create a "quarrelsome day" plan. Choose exactly what you'll have the children do as far as education on those days. You might even want to create a menu as well of easy to prepare or already prepared meals to have on hand at all times for when a quarrelsome funk settles over your house. Finally, make sure to pray often on days when everything seems to have a dark cloud over it. Petition God's help in getting things back to normal the next day.

Week 8

And he said to them, "Come away by yourselves to a desolate place and rest a while."
For many were coming and going, and they had no leisure even to eat.

—Mark 6:31

Probably the most difficult aspect of being a homeschool mom is that you are always surrounded with so much coming and going all day long as a mom and/or a teacher. Our children don't leave home to go to school, unlike other stay-at-home moms, and most of us don't work outside the home either. While we made this choice, and most of the time enjoy our decision, one important thing to remember is that you need time for you. In the verse above, Jesus is reminding His apostles that no matter how important your work is for God, you still need time for you.

So how is a homeschool mom supposed to find time for herself? The key is that you don't find it, you make it happen, just like Jesus made His apostles.

Every Day

The first hurdle is to carve out some time every day for you. Susan Wise Bauer of The Well-Trained Mind required her children to have a two-hour quiet time every day. Each child would go to their own room and spend the two hours listening to audio books, reading, or finishing school work, but they had to leave mom and each other alone for that time. Her plan gives everyone a chance to have some downtime. I find my snippet of daily me time at the end of the day. My husband takes over the prepping for bedtime duties, and I snuggle myself into bed early and read or watch TV. Other homeschool moms I know have their daily time while exercising for an hour or spending time at the local coffee shop.

Weekly

For many years my oldest daughter was involved in an extracurricular activity that took us out of the house for two to three hours every week. I valued that time so much! I would drop her off and proceed to the nearest library where I curled up and read books and wrote out blog posts. It was sheer bliss and a great way to have guaranteed me time every week while my husband took care of the younger two for me. However, this past year, we dropped the extracurricular that provided my regular weekly me time. Suddenly, I had no weekly time to myself. After six months of this, I couldn't' take it anymore. I needed that time back to be a good mother and homeschooler. I finally just told my husband I needed him to find two hours in his weekly schedule where I could disappear off by myself. He named a day and a time, and before I knew it, I had my me time back. It doesn't need to be a huge chunk of time, but do try to trade off babysitting with another mom or leave your husband in charge and head off to be alone every week or two.

Monthly

I don't really do anything for myself monthly. Since I have my weekly time alone, I've not found it necessary. However, I do know of homeschool co-ops that schedule a monthly mom's night out, or you could schedule one with some close friends. Maybe your church has a ladies' activity every month in which you want to participate. Or possibly you take time every month to go to the nail salon and have a mani/pedi. Whatever it is, carve out time every month for yourself if you can't manage to do it every week.

Yearly

I'm not going to lie. I protect my yearly alone time with a vengeance. It's only happened the past two years, but I've loved it so much I'm trying to make it keep happening for the foreseeable future. Every year I get an entire week alone. All the members of my family go off to various scheduled pursuits, and I stay at home for seven blissful days of nothing but me time. I know that this is probably not possible for most women, but try to find a day or two that you could be alone every year. Homeschool conventions are great for this. You can go by yourself or with a small group of friends and shop curriculum, talk about homeschooling, and rejuvenate for the coming year. Plus, it helps you feel productive about taking time away from home just for you.

I've found that without a doubt I am a happier, more loving, and more peaceful wife and mother when I get scheduled time alone. It gives me a chance to disengage from the family for a short while and fill up my own tank with things I enjoy and love before returning to them rested in mind and soul. I truly believe it is much more of a necessity than most moms think.

Diagnosis:
When was the last time you had any time to yourself? If you can't remember or it's been longer than three months, it's been too long!

Why do you think Jesus recognized the need in his apostles, and in us, for time spent alone?

Sometimes I encounter women who seem to think that trying to find me time makes you a bad person or an unloving wife or mother. Do you agree or disagree? Why or why not?

Prescription:
Right now, during this off week from school, come up with a plan to create daily time for yourself, and begin to implement it this week so that your children, your spouse, and you can get used to it. Also talk to your spouse or another mom about creating weekly or monthly time alone. Put this date or dates on your calendar and protect that time as something fixed and unchangeable. Start researching and planning for some yearly getaway for yourself as well.

Week 9

I am the Lord your God, who brought you out of the land of Egypt, out of the house of slavery. You shall have no other gods before me. —Exodus 20:2-3

I am going to touch on something that I've seen hints of in the Christian home-school community. Please don't scoff or assume this doesn't apply to you because I believe all of us, including myself, have fallen victim to this trap: making homeschooling an idol.

While I know homeschool moms aren't creating statues of curriculum to worship, I suspect most of us in the dark recesses of our mind trust that our decision to homeschool will lead to children that follow in our faith. In other words, we're hedging our bets that homeschooling our children creates Christian children. In a nutshell, that's creating an idol— trusting in something other than God to save us.

So here's a quick litmus test to see if you are anchoring your child's salvation to homeschooling.

Does the idea of sending your children to public school immediately cause you to doubt if your children would become Christians?

It's easy to look at the perils that exist in public schools, from curriculum choices to bullying, to school violence to peer pressure, and assume that there is no way a child could make it through that gauntlet with their faith unscathed. If you look at statistics, you would be even more fearful. However, God doesn't need perfect circumstances to save your child. Daniel and his friends were able to stay faithful while living in the palace of a world leader who was anything but godly. While the challenges are definitely more in a public school setting for the Christian family, it doesn't mean that their ticket to heaven is revoked. You might have to work more at keeping Christ as the focus of your child's life, but external circumstances have never been dependent upon God's arm to save. Not to mention, I know plenty of homeschool children who did not turn out the way their parents had hoped.

Do you secretly look at Christian families whose children attend public school and feel sorry for them and worry about the souls of their children?

When it seems like you are attacked from all sides about your choice to home-school, comments from strangers, disbelieving family and friends, how homeschooling is portrayed in media, it's hard not to become a champion for homeschooling to those who don't. Crossing the line into judging and becoming prideful about your decision to homeschool is a big no-no. We all know the Bible speaks very negatively about pride. When you place homeschooling as an idol, then it's very easy to look at others who don't homeschool and assume a lot of things about them. They don't want to live on one income so that's why they don't homeschool (assuming they are greedy and/or selfish). They won't even consider homeschooling because they don't want their children to miss out on the school experience (assuming the school experience consists of sinful things that you would never expose your child to, or that the school experience is more important than their children's souls). The list could go on and on. I leave you with one verse from the book of Proverbs, "Pride goes before destruction, and a haughty spirit before a fall" (16:18). Don't see homeschooling as something that saves, and you won't have a problem with pride and judging others.

Do you sometimes treat raising your children as a recipe where following all the steps leads to faithful, Christian children with homeschooling being the main ingredient in this recipe?
As all Christian parents, we desire our children to continue in the faith, but it becomes very easy to try to control every variable we can think of to insure this outcome. We make rules about modesty, rules about media and entertainment, surround our children with only Christian friends, explain what is expected about dating or courting, and we homeschool. "Surely," we think, "if I control all these aspects of their lives, if I keep them as protected as possible, if I manipulate situations and events so my child is insulated from as much worldliness as possible, then I am certain they will be Christians." Nothing is wrong with doing these things or having standards for your home. The problem is your motivation. Are you trying to help God with your child's salvation, or are you merely living a Christian life before your children as best you can? There is a fine line between the two, but there is a difference. Abraham and Sarah also tried to help God out with His promise of a son, and we all know how that turned out. God doesn't need your help to save your children; He needs parents who trust Him and live a Christian life.

This entry might seem in direct contradiction to others in this book, but it's not. I want us to examine our motivation for why we do what we do. Are you coming from a place of fear or from a place of faith? A place of conviction or a place of control? Your motivation matters to God.

Diagnosis:
Did you answer any of these questions in the affirmative, or have you found yourself thinking thoughts similar to these at different times?

Why do you think it's easy to fall into the trap of seeing homeschooling as a way to save our children?

Prescription:
First, pray for forgiveness if this has been a struggle for you, or pray for protection if it hasn't. Read and respond to these verses as they pertain to viewing homeschooling as an idol: Jeremiah 29:11; Matthew 19:26; Isaiah 55:8-11; John 16:33.

Week 10

Be imitators of me, as I am of Christ. —1 Corinthians 11:1

About four years ago, I was complaining to my husband about how much the children yelled and screamed at each other. It was annoying and really rude. My husband said something that really was necessary, but difficult to hear. He pointed out that I yelled and screamed at them a lot as well, and quite possibly, their behavior was merely a reflection of my own. Ouch, that hurt. However, he was absolutely correct. Our children watch and imitate us, and there are many times I wish it wasn't true. My goal is the verse above. I want to be able to tell my children those words and live up to them.

One of the cruel ironies of life is that you cannot give what you don't already possess. If I wish for my children to have quiet, kind voices when interacting with each other, then I need to do the same. If I wish for my children to not complain about math, then I need to be able to be excited about math as well, even if I have to fake it. If I want a homeschool characterized by gentleness and patience, then I need to be that for my children. Unfortunately, if I don't already possess the character traits I want my children to exhibit, then I must remedy that default posthaste.

Once upon a time in the United States, schools recognized the influence teachers imparted to their students when it came to morality. The following quotation is from Thomas Stockwell, Commissioner of Public Schools, when asked to report about morals in public schools:

> "I think that the main force to be relied upon for the promotion of moral culture is not so much a system of ethics or a well-organized plan of instruction, as the life which the teacher lives before the pupils. The most effective means for implanting the seed of virtue and including a sound morality are often the almost unconscious words and acts of the sincere and faithful teacher, which are, as it were, the spontaneous overflow of his own pure character."

Did you catch that? The most important force to teach morals to children is the unconscious actions and words we use while teaching.

While these ideas are antiquated by modern standards, they are complementary to the verse above. We are the Christian example our children witness. We are who they are modeling their morals and character upon as our own character overflows throughout the day. When they struggle, what do our unconscious actions and overflow of character say? When they disobey, what do our unconscious actions and overflow of character say? As much as I wish it weren't true, I fear that many times I want my children to do anything but imitate me.

Diagnosis:
What are you giving your children to imitate?

If Jesus homeschooled (since we are supposed to be imitating Him), what do you think His unconscious words and acts would be like while teaching His children? How does that differ from your words and actions?

Prescription:
I'm sure we all know ways in which our lives do not mirror the standard of Jesus. This week, think specifically of the ways you fall short while homeschooling. Choose just three of those to really focus on this week while parenting your children. If it's patience, really try to be more patient with your children. It it's encouragement, try to be more encouraging. Make sure when you start back to school that you continue working on various character traits throughout the weeks to come.

Week 11

The heart is deceitful above all things, and desperately sick; who can understand it?
—Jeremiah 17:9

Do you ever doubt yourself and your ability to homeschool? Do you believe those feelings? In the verse above "the heart" refers to our feelings. Feelings are deceitful and many times, especially as women, trying to understand why we are feeling a certain way is almost impossible. Satan loves to use our feelings against us to make us ineffective and weak, especially in an area like homeschooling where we already feel uncertain and the heavy weight of responsibility. That's why it's even more important to be careful not to allow false feelings to derail our homeschools. Let's explore some common feelings associated with homeschooling and how to speak truth in the face of those lies.

Urgency: "Rush, rush, rush! Hurry and get through the day! Pound the information in their head because a fourth grader is supposed to know how to do this. We don't have time to play a game; get back to the table." Probably one of the most common feelings to homeschool moms is the feeling of urgency. We have so much to teach and so little time to fit it all. And that, folks, is the lie. You don't have so much to teach because you can't teach it all to start with, and you don't have a little time. You have 13 years at a minimum. I decided long ago that my goal with math and my oldest daughter is to have her complete the bare minimum requirement to go to college by the time she's 18. That gives us plenty of time to work at her pace without frustration and anger taking over our math time together. I'd rather that she truly learns and understands math, than rush her based on some manmade timetable of academic goals and ruin our relationship in the process. ***Home education is a marathon, not a sprint.***

Fear: "I'm going to ruin my kids' lives. They will not learn everything they need to know. They will be failures, and it will be all my fault. They will be behind!" Hey, homeschool mom, you're falling for it again. That same old hook that snagged Eve way back in the beginning: You are not God. You do not have so much power over your child's life that you can singlehandedly ruin it or cause them to fail, nor can you teach them everything they need to know because you don't even know what they will need in the future since you don't know the future! As for getting behind, behind whom? They are exactly where God wants them to be. You be faithful in teaching your children about this world and the world to come. God will take care of the rest. ***Home education is nothing to fear with the Lord teaching, instructing, and guiding along with you.***

Stress: "I can't do it all. The house is never clean, the laundry is always behind, and I never cook dinner anymore. Not to mention that I'm supposed to educate the children and chauffer them around to their extra-curricular activities. I'm so stressed!" Homeschooling is a full time job by itself, and when you add in all of the other stay-at-home mom duties, it is even more on top of that. Don't let Satan drag you down with this stressful feeling. He wants you to focus on how long your days are and how it seems like you are just spinning your wheels. The truth is that, as someone once so eloquently put it, **the days are long, but the years are short.** One day, before you know it, all of this craziness will come to an end, and then you can manage everything to your wishes. Right now, focus on the education side of things and work to reduce your stress in the other areas by lowering your standards and involving others.

Inadequacy: "I'm not a good homeschool mom. I don't ever do fun things with my children. They hate being homeschooled, and it's because I'm such a horrible teacher. All of the other homeschool moms never have these kinds of problems. Did you see on Instagram that awesome art project Mary's kids did? I could never do something like that." Ahhh, the old comparison trap, another snare of the wily Devil. Anytime you get involved in a comparison war you will always come out the loser. Why? Because you are comparing your everyday life to someone else's highlight reel that you see via social media, blogs, etc. There is nothing wrong with you. You are the perfect teacher for your children just the way you are. **God gave your children to you because you are what your children need.** Be confident in that fact, and don't compare yourself, your children, or your homeschool to any other.

I only chose these four feelings, but I could easily have doubled this list, because we've all been there. I promise you that if you let these deceitful feelings hang around too long, you will start to believe them, and when you start to believe them, you will act on them. Usually that leads to all kinds of negative behaviors on your part and a home and homeschool that feel the wrath of mom more than her gentleness. Don't let your desperately sick heart set the tone of your homeschool.

Diagnosis:
What negative feelings have you found creeping into your thoughts about homeschooling or yourself as a homeschool mom?

How have negative feelings manifested themselves in your homeschool days?

Prescription:
Write a self-affirmation sentence or paragraph using the bolded sentences above as your jumping off point. Read it every day before starting your school time this year. We need this truth daily to counteract those lies we feel about ourselves.

Week 12

For am I now seeking the approval of man, or of God? Or am I trying to please man? If I were still trying to please man, I would not be a servant of Christ. —Galatians 1:10

There are few decisions made by families that seem to invite more criticism than when they decide to homeschool. Close family, extended family, friends, church family, and even total strangers feel perfectly justified in commenting about such a personal decision. Most comments are encouraging and supportive, but occasionally someone tries to dissuade you from your decision by pointing out various ways your children will be crippled for life. Usually if it's a stranger, criticism is easy to brush off, but when family and friends make hurtful, disparaging comments, it can create tension between normally positive relationships.

The apostle Paul knew quite a bit about life decisions resulting in people turning on you. Once he became a Christian, his previous comrades sought to kill him (Acts 9:23-25). In the verse above, Paul shares his wisdom in dealing with critics. Ultimately to overcome those who criticize, we need to remember three points: seek God's approval, don't try to please others, and be a servant of Christ.

Seek God' Approval

If you have made the decision to homeschool, then you have probably been convicted this is what God wants for your family. You have prayed about your decision, you have researched, you have considered the pros and cons, and chosen to homeschool. Go forward, knowing God will guide you along it. He approves of what you are doing, and that's the only opinion which matters in the end.

Don't Try to Please Others

Abraham Lincoln is famous for saying, "You can please all of the people some of the time and some of the people all of the time, but you can't please all of the people all of the time." No matter how close to you the people criticizing are, you need to remember that ultimately their opinion of how you educate your children is not their decision. God gave your children to you to raise, not anyone else. Pleasing others never trumps God's approval or God's will for your family. And as Lincoln pointed out, trying to please everyone is a losing proposition.

Be a Servant of Christ

No matter how painful criticism and disparaging comments are, as a servant of Christ, there is an appropriate response.

Seek to inform. Often people criticize what they don't understand. Assume the best about people that they really need to understand how homeschooling works to get on board. Have a question and answer session so they can ask you about specific concerns they might have about homeschooling. Educate them about home education.

Be respectful. Even after you've explained home schooling, if they still are critical of your decision, be respectful and do not lose your temper. No one is ever won over with harsh words.

Establish firm boundaries. Don't continue the argument about your decision to homeschool. Let the people in your life that continue to be critical know that trying to dissuade you from homeschooling is not a topic of conversation. Your family has made its decision, and that is the end of any discussion. If they continue to try to bring up the topic, then change the conversation.

Sometimes this criticism can become extreme to the point where people are going behind your back and start trying to persuade your children to beg you to enroll them in school. If the critics in your life begin undermining your authority with your children or making rude, cutting remarks to you in the presence of others, it is time to consider not having a relationship with those people anymore. Know your conviction and move forward.

Diagnosis:
How do you know homeschooling is what you're supposed to be doing?

Have you ever received criticism for your decision to homeschool? Did it make you question yourself?

Are there any people in your life who consistently criticize homeschooling?

Prescription:
Create "conversation stop" phrases and memorize them so when people feel the need to comment about homeschooling in a negative way, you're ready. I've included a list below of questions I've been asked, or other homeschoolers I know have been asked, to get you started on creating your phrases.

What about socialization?
How will you teach high school?
Is homeschooling even legal?
How do you do it? I could never homeschool!
What about prom, sports, band, etc.?
How will your children be prepared for the real world?
You can't shelter your kids forever, you know.

Week 13

For you formed my inward parts, you knitted me together in my mother's womb. I praise you, for I am fearfully and wonderfully made. —Psalm 139:13-14a

Charlotte Mason, a British educator at the turn of the century whose methods are popular in homeschool circles, had a revolutionary thought. She espoused that children are born persons. This idea was the total opposite of prevailing educational theory at the time, which espoused children came into the world as blank slates needing to be filled with knowledge by parents and teachers.

The idea of children as born persons is supported by the verses above as well. Children aren't born as blank slates, but as human beings made in God's image by God himself. They are born with their own personalities, talents, and curiosity about the world.

So how does this apply to our homeschools?

Don't put your children in an educational box.
I don't know if this means God has a sense of humor, but inevitably it seems we all have at least one child, possibly more, who is totally different than we are. For example, my oldest is super artistic and crafty. She loves hands-on learning, experiments, and projects. All of that sounds like torture to me. I once failed an assignment in a required high school art class because I couldn't draw a straight line with a ruler! As for hands-on learning and experiments, I'd much rather read a book about it. I quickly discovered that trying to fit her into my style of learning was not going to work. Don't misunderstand me; she enjoys a good book, but she'd much rather make and do after she's read about something than write about it. I tried for a year to force her to learn the way I like to learn. Why? Because it's easier for me to teach, it's easier for me to plan, it's more enjoyable for me. The result was a year of misery for my oldest and a hard lesson for me to learn. She is a person who has her own style and talents. I must respect that because God made her that way, and even if I don't understand it, He has use for her in His kingdom.

Don't compare your children to others.
We all know how detrimental this can be for not only our children, but ourselves as well. You meet a child who is light years ahead of your own struggling writer, and you begin to panic. Your youngest child struggles with reading, and you don't understand why. Their older sibling was reading by this age. While comparison sometimes helps you determine if there could possibly be some underlying learning challenges, for the most part it's a dangerous and destructive path to walk. Your child is walking their own path in this world, not the path of the super genius you read about on the internet, not the path of their siblings, not the path of the children sitting in their desks at the local public school. Once you acknowledge that your children are born persons, it's easier to let those expectations go and

watch their own lives and gifts unfold before your very eyes.

Don't take full responsibility for their learning.
Probably my biggest fault during this homeschool venture has been allowing myself to get too emotionally entangled in my children's education. When I base my feelings of self-worth on the successes and failures of our homeschool day, I'm in big trouble. The fact that my youngest child struggles with phonics is not a reflection of my worth. It does not make me a bad person or a failure. It means I have a little boy who is going to need some extra help to learn how to read.

Viewing your child as a creation of God, a blessing given to your family, means that God saw fit to give this child to you to raise and teach. He didn't give you this child as a way to punish you or point out how lacking you are. It's totally ridiculous to even think that, but when our worth rises and falls with the educational successes and failures of our children, that's basically what we're saying. Your children will learn what they need to know to achieve the things God has planned for them. It might not be on the time table you wish, it might require outside intervention for learning disabilities, and it might send you to your knees in prayer for guidance and patience multiple times a day, but it does not reflect on your worth as a person or your capability as a teacher.

Diagnosis:
Do you find yourself projecting your style of learning on your children? Has it caused any trouble in your homeschool?

Have you been guilty of comparing your child to other children their age or their siblings? Is that fair to your child?

Why do we let our value become entangled with our children's educational abilities?

Prescription:
Make a list for each child of their talents, interests, preferred learning methods, etc. Now think of ways you could incorporate these into your homeschool curriculum and jot down some ideas. When you start school back, use one or two of them with your child. Some examples of things I've done:

● Let my creative child make a stop motion video of the assassination of Julius Caesar using her American Girl dolls.
● Used my son's dump truck to pick up the number of blocks from the floor on the number flashcard and drive the blocks to me so I can check if he got the load correct.
● My math-loving girl used Minecraft to build the animal habitats we studied in science.

Week 14

For He will hide me in his shelter in the day of trouble; he will conceal me under the cover of his tent; he will lift me high upon a rock. —Psalm 27:5

In our culture, the context of sheltering is almost always viewed negatively. Saying that someone is sheltered brings to mind a person with no common sense, no idea of how the real world works, and they are stunted in their growth into adulthood because of it. However, the biblical view of sheltering is totally different.

In the Bible, sheltering is almost always used in the context of protection and safety, as illustrated in the verse above penned by David, and it is something we should seek and desire. When you are a homeschooler, you are in the blessed position of being able to shelter your children from worldly forces. To give them a place of safety and protection from the evil that is around them. You are able to provide a place for them to learn without hearing teaching that is contrary to your faith. You are able to associate with other children whose family values are aligned with yours. You are able to build up their defenses where they are weak and encourage their strengths without outside influences that might be contrary to those goals.

When a young man or young woman decides to join the military, they are immediately "sheltered" by them. They are given clothing, food, housing, and training. All of this is done for one end goal: to prepare them for battle. They are removed from the general population and given focused, intense training so that if they are ever faced with combat, they know how to react instinctively. When you homeschool, you are pulling your child out of the general population to train them spiritually, mentally, emotionally, and academically for life.

If you homeschool, you've probably been asked if your children will turn into a socially awkward child, or what some in society calls weird kids— you know, children that may be a little different than all the other kids. On one hand, I fervently hope that my children will be weird and different than other kids their age, especially when it comes to their morality and Christian walk. On the other hand, I want them to be prepared for life on their own and a faith of their own. I don't want them to be crippled because I homeschooled them.

I am determined to make sure that my children are prepared for life, not sheltered from it. I want them trained in how to defend their faith (1 Peter 3:15). I want them to learn how to be a godly husband or wife, how to take care of the home and their children, how to be a leader in the home, how to submit, how to respect. I want them to have the practical skills of being able to fill out a job application and go on job interviews. I want them to know how to budget, how to grocery shop for healthy, filling foods, how to figure interest, how to do basic home and automotive repairs, how to garden, etc. I want them to have the skills to find information that they need, to read a map, to carry on conversations eloquently and knowledgeably, and to deal with bullies (this group exists well into adulthood!).

When you homeschool, you are able to experience the beautiful concept of Biblical sheltering. You provide a safe, protected environment to learn how to manage life, faith, and family. We've already had to deal with some bullying despite homeschooling, but we were able to hold off on encountering it until the third grade when my oldest was able to understand what was happening and what her response should be. We've dealt with science and history books whose viewpoints we don't agree with, but I was able to present those things to my children when I chose to do so because I knew they were ready to handle it without compromising their growing faith in God.

The beauty of the homeschooling lifestyle is that, for the most part, my husband and I get to make those choices and decisions. We decided when to open the shelter of our family and deal with ugly, sinful things. The blessing of homeschooling is that my children are protected from having to deal with more weighty matters until they have the tools to do so. They are protected from having to hear certain academic teachings until they are grounded in the truth. They are safe from sinful social issues until we decide to explain those things to them.

I feel blessed that homeschooling gives us the opportunity to shelter them in the Lord until they are ready to be unleashed on the world and ready for battle. So if someone tells you that your children will be sheltered or weird because you homeschool them, smile really broadly, and give them a genuine, "We hope so!"

Diagnosis:
Have you ever had someone question your decision to homeschool by pointing out that you would be sheltering your child or they would be weird? How did you react?

Why do you think being sheltered is viewed so negatively in our culture?

What positives can come from sheltering? Of what negatives do you need to be wary?

Prescription:
List some specific blessings you've seen from sheltering your own children from peer and societal influences. As an example, one of the greatest compliments I ever received about our decision to homeschool came from a teenage girl at our church. She stopped me in the hallway one Sunday morning and told me that she thought it was cool how Grace, our oldest, was so comfortable being who she was and liking the things she liked without worrying about fitting in or being teased. She told me that sometimes she wished she'd been homeschooled so she didn't worry so much about what others thought. That was a benefit of sheltering I'd never thought about before.

Week 15

In the fear of the Lord one has strong confidence, and his children will have refuge.
—Proverbs 14:26

When I first started contemplating the idea of homeschooling, I had one huge fear: teaching my children to read. I didn't even remember learning how to read myself. As my oldest is now approaching high school, an entirely new set of fears are appearing. The fact that I succeeded at teaching two children to read so far has taught me some things in the confidence department to help me face my new worries.

I have confidence that I can learn with my child in order to teach my child. Even though I've taken algebra once in my life, I'm already working through an algebra book to refresh my memory so that I'm prepared for the coming years. I also learn things every day while educating the kids. Can you believe that I didn't know the difference between long vowel sounds and short vowels sounds before I taught my oldest to read?!? Have confidence in your ability to learn!

I have confidence that I know when to outsource my teaching. Sometimes it doesn't matter how much I try, there are some subjects beyond my confidence zone. I'm looking at you, geometry and physics! Thankfully there are multiple DVD options, online options, tutors, and co-op options to handle just about any subject you fear. It is a great time to be home educating with such a wide range of choices on exactly how to teach. Have confidence that you know when you need some extra help!

I have confidence that I can research to find the best curriculum for my children and me. One of the first things I tell someone when they mention they are thinking about homeschooling is "Whatever you do, don't do an internet search for homeschool curriculum!" We live in a day when homeschool curriculum is plentiful, almost too plentiful. But one great thing about having so many choices is that with a little research among homeschool friends, online reviews, and good old trial and error, you can be confident that you find something that will help you teach almost any subject to almost any child.

I have confidence in God. I saved this one until the end because it is the most important of all. When you are called to homeschool, when you know it is God's will for your family to home educate, it can be easy to believe that you will struggle because you are not a professional teacher. I want to let you know, as someone who earned a degree in education, that if you have the Lord, you have the strength and the power of the best teacher that ever walked the earth. In 1 John 5:14-15, it even says that our confidence can be found in knowing that what we ask, when it's aligned with His will, it is heard and answered. Have confidence in our God, for He listens and answers our petitions!

Diagnosis:
In what area or areas do you feel most confident to teach your child?

What practical ways can you brainstorm to increase your confidence in the subjects you feel the least confident?

Prescription:
Stop right now and pray to God for confidence in those areas that He will lead you to the right curriculum, that He will lead you to the right resources, and that He will help you learn. While you're at it, pray for confidence in all of your subjects. One thing that helps me feel more confident is to have a plan. Choose one of the subjects you are least confident about teaching, and create a game plan for how you will address that subject as your children get older. As an example, here's my plan for upper level science: I am going to find a co-op, cottage school, or university model school to enroll the kids in for high school science. If that fails, I will use DVD learning or an online class. My third option is to find another homeschool family or families and do upper level science together. Now create your own plan.

Week 16

I can do all things through him who strengthens me. —Philippians 4:13

I can

Don't listen to the naysayers out there or your own doubts. You ARE capable of teaching your children all the way from kindergarten through senior year in high school. How do I know? Because I know you are a mom who loves God and loves her children. When those two things are true, I know you will do your best to provide educational opportunities and good curriculum for your child, and above all else, you will teach them to love the Lord. You can...

Do all things

It may take some trial and error, but you can figure out how to complete the necessary requirements to educate your children at home. At times it may seem impossible, especially if you have little ones, to envision a moment when everyone is learning, housework is relatively caught up, and meals are more home-cooked than takeout, but you'll get there. One thing is certain though, none of it will be perfect, so don't stress over achieving that goal, because you are doing it all...

Through Him

You can't achieve success any other way unless you place your anchor on Him. You are a weak, imperfect person, but when you give everything to him and ask him to guide you, then great things will happen. You will never have enough, but He will make it abundant. You will never know enough, but He will make you wise. You will never feel that you are enough, but He will show you that isn't true, because it is Jesus...

Who strengthens me

No one can do it on their own without the strength of the Lord. On days when it all seems hopeless, pointless, and useless, He steps in to remind us that the difficult times are when we grow. God cares deeply about your homeschool and loves your children far more than you do. He wants you to succeed so He has no problem giving you and your family all they need to grow in wisdom and in His love.

All of the above is true of course, but it does require us to do one thing: humble ourselves. Instead of making plans for your child's academic future or following what a curriculum tells you to do for the year and then asking God to bless those plans, what if you asked God what His plans are for your children and your homeschool, and to help you follow His lead. Do you see the difference in the humble attitude? God gives strength to those who are weak (2 Corinthians 12:10) not to those who believe they have it all figured out. In the same vein as Mark 9:24, I humble myself to receive your strength! Jesus, help my prideful heart!

Diagnosis:
Do you truly believe you can homeschool? Why or why not?

Why do we need Jesus to homeschool well?

How can pride keep Jesus out of our homeschool if we aren't careful?

Prescription:
Make a commitment to God that you will follow His lead in your homeschool. When plans go awry, look for the lesson He wants you to learn about yourself or your children. When doubts sweep in, turn to Him for strength and guidance. Make both a verbal commitment through prayer and written commitment in the space below.

CPSIA information can be obtained
at www.ICGtesting.com
Printed in the USA
FFOW04n1102140817
38729FF